from hurting to happy
from hurting to happy
from hurting to happy

Praise for *From Hurting to Happy*

"As an author of true histories for young people, I appreciate how readers can learn from someone else's story. Through the stories she tells, Barbara Bartocci shares her wisdom, advising and comforting as she helps us work through ordinary and extraordinary losses in our lives. To read her book is to have a friend along for the journey."

◆ **ANDREA WARREN**, author of the Booker Award winner, *Orphan Train Rider*, as well as *Surviving Hitler* and *More Stories About Orphan Train Riders*

"We all need something positive to help us move on following the loss of hopes, dreams, significant others in our lives. In this personal and empathic work, Barbara Bartocci offers much-needed direction and hope."

◆ **CLAIRE BERMAN**, best-selling author of *Caring for Yourself While Caring for Your Aging Parents*

"Barbara Bartocci has written a book that soars with hope, and could only come from someone who has, herself, experienced losses. Everyone can benefit from her insights."

◆ **ANTOINETTE BOSCO**, author of Christopher Award-winning *Choosing Mercy: A Mother of Murder Victims Pleads to End the Death Penalty*

from hurting to happy
from hurting to happy
from **hurting** to happy

Transforming
Your Life
After
Loss

Barbara Bartocci

SORIN BOOKS   Notre Dame, Indiana

---

www.sorinbooks.com

International Standard Book Number: 1-893732-54-1

Cover photograph © Halli Freireich/Workbook Co/Op Stock

Cover and text design by Katherine Robinson Coleman

Printed and bound in the United States of America.

Library of Congress Cataloging-in-Publication Data

Bartocci, Barbara.

     From hurting to happy : transforming your life after loss / Barbara Bartocci.
     p. cm.
Includes bibliographical references.
     ISBN 1-893732-54-1 (pbk.)
  1. Loss (Psychology) 2. Loss (Psychology)--Religious aspects--Christianity. 3. Grief. 4. Grief--Religious aspects--Christianity. I. Title.
     BF575.D35 B37 2002
     155.9'3--dc21

                                2002003131
                                   CIP

Acknowledgments

Gratefully, I acknowledge all those whose stories appear in this book and who, by sharing, will inspire and encourage others. I give thanks for permission to use quotes and to reference other authors, and I encourage my readers to peruse my list of resource books. I was personally touched by all of the books I name.

Special appreciation to my local "in-house" editors, Tina Hacker, Sony Hocklander, Deborah Shouse, and Andrea Warren. I couldn't have done it without you!

And many thanks to Robert Hamma, book editor par excellence, who is so professional yet also so understanding and sensitive to authors.

Thanks also to my fine colleagues in the American Society of Journalists and Authors, and to my Kansas City writer friends. Your encouragement has meant so much.

Finally, but never last or least, Jim Todd has my special thanks and love.

Contents

Introduction:
Rediscovering Joy After Loss

*T*he heavy lunch crush had ended, so the restaurant was quiet when I walked in, and I quickly spotted Amy in a booth near the back. She was younger than I, with red Orphan Annie curls and, usually, a wide smile. I headed her way, still curious about why she had called. We had only met a few times, mostly in business situations.

As I slid into the booth, she smiled, though her eyes looked suspiciously damp. Had she been crying?

Our waiter came. Ice tinkled as Amy sipped her water. Through the window I noticed some cheerful geraniums in a pot on the patio. Suddenly, Amy blurted, "Barbara, how do you manage to be so happy?"

Taken aback, my mouth dropped open. "Happy?"

She nodded. "You've had plenty of things go wrong in your life. I've read your books, so I know. And yet . . ." two fat tears slid down her cheeks. She gulped and almost couldn't continue. "I don't think I can ever be happy again." Weeping, she told me how her husband had just walked out of their marriage. Only two months ago, her father had died in a car crash. "The two men I loved the most in this world—and now they're both gone. . . ."

The waiter approached with our salads. I waved him off and reached for Amy's hand. I wanted to put my arms around her, and soothe her with a promise that everything would be all right.

For truly, I believed it would.

But I knew from experience how much it hurts to lose someone you love, or have a situation end that you thought would last forever. So for a while, I simply held her hand, and remembered some of the times when I shook *my* fist at God—and life—because something or someone dear was taken from me.

And I reflected on how to answer her question.

Maybe it's your question too. How *do* you become happy again? How do you work your way through the pain, fear, sadness, and sometimes *rage* that accompany the different kinds of loss that assault us in life? On a spiritual level, how do you regain your trust in God when some overwhelming—and unfair—loss invades your life?

I once saw a psychological scale that measures the stress level of change. It said the three hardest are (1) death of a spouse or child, (2) divorce, and (3) losing your job.

In my own life, I've been widowed, divorced, and fired from a job.

I lost both of my parents, who died fairly young.

All three of my children had special needs growing up.

At different times, I lost my role and my place in my community.

And, just as painful in its own way, I lost my image of what I thought life *should* be.

For a while, I lost my faith in God.

And when clinical depression overtook me, I even briefly pondered losing my own life. Yet I know I'm not unique. Losses pile up in everyone's life. No one escapes—not even the "rich and famous"—because loss is part of living. (Although for many years, I fantasized that some magical place existed where instead of ups and downs, certain lucky people experienced only ups and upper-ups.)

Amy desperately wanted to know *how* you move beyond grief and pain.

I understood. I remember wondering once how I could feel so much pain when it was not my body that was bloody and rent apart, but my soul. How could emotion—something you can't touch or see—hurt *so much*?

She asked how I stay so happy, but *happy* is not quite the right word. It's more an inner joy; a feeling of peace and a trust in God's presence—in *all* circumstances—that I feel today.

And it's been a long time coming.

Is there a guide—a process you can take to make grief transformational rather than defeating?

I believe there is, and I'd like to be your guide. In this book I will tell the stories—from my life and the lives of others—that show how you can go through loss and emerge whole on the other side. And how God is there even when the mist of grief obscures your view.

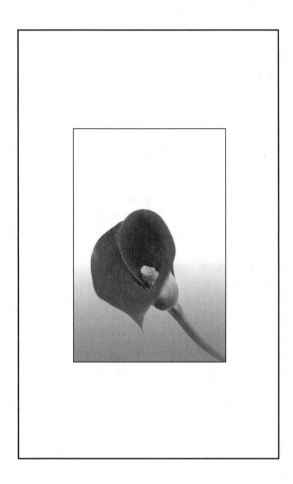

1.

Saying Good-Bye

The web of our life is of mingled yarn,
good and ill together.

William Shakespeare

When loss occurs, you embark on a journey, and the journey begins with a farewell. You are leaving behind someone you loved, a situation you knew, or the person you were. Saying good-bye is difficult, often painful, and for many it stretches over time; but unless you say good-bye, you can't move forward.

I have learned that people's stories of saying good-bye share common threads of emotion. You can learn from another person's story, even if their circumstances differ from your own.

Good-byes must be faced and—yes—embraced, before you take the next step in the healing process.

Sudden Loss

The loss that washed over me like a tidal wave, throwing me under to gasp and wonder if I would drown, occurred when I was twenty-nine. It was Labor Day weekend, 1968. My parents, three children, and I were returning to Southern California from a week's visit with my grandmother in Colorado.

Our trip had offered a welcome respite.

My husband John, a Navy fighter pilot, was flying in combat in Vietnam. It was his second combat cruise, and in 1968, the air war was ferocious. Many pilots had been killed or captured as POWs. It was hard work to keep my fear at bay.

My parents lived about an hour and a half from San Diego, where John and I lived. As we pulled into their driveway at the end of our trip, my father murmured, "I don't recognize that car." In the gathering dusk, we peered at the white Buick that sat parked in their driveway.

Two shadowy forms got out of the car and I saw my Navy friends, Bob and his wife, Irene. Abruptly, the world slowed. I experienced a vivid awareness of each small motion—Bob's mouth opening wide, his hand reaching out, Irene's arm sliding around my shoulders, my mother's horrified stare, my father's slight stumble as he took in the news.

Softly, Bob spoke. John was dead. His plane had crashed as he tried to bring it aboard the carrier after a night mission over North Vietnam. His body was lost at sea.

We had been married for ten years—my entire adult life—and our children were still young: nine, seven, and five. What I didn't know then, in the anguish of that night, was that I had only begun my journey of loss. John's death marked the beginning of hundreds of painful changes, big and small, in my life and my children's.

a helping hand

At one moment, your life is proceeding as usual. In a single instant, everything is changed. You inhabit a different world. It's a world beyond anything you formerly knew, loved, possessed, expected. You can't grasp it. Time slows. Your mind goes numb. Physically, you may scream or abruptly go mute and be unable to speak. Your body may feel pierced by thousands of tiny, razor-sharp daggers. Or your skin may tingle as if on fire. You can't breathe. A veil falls over your eyes, and everything darkens. Or you see small details with incredible clarity. You sway, and possibly fall. Or faint.

Shock and denial lay first claim when a major loss occurs. You're like an infant, unable to think or act rationally. Shock is a blessing. It numbs your emotional pain center in the same way it would numb third-degree burns. You need time to absorb a shattering new reality.

Realize that all major loss is understood incrementally. No one absorbs it all at once. In the very beginning, you can only let go and allow others to lift you, trusting that someone will hold your head above the crashing waves of pain.

Early Response

In the immediate wake of learning my husband was dead, I did two things: I went to a movie and I went to church.

A movie? Yes. We learned of John's death on a Friday night and planned to drive to San Diego from my parents' home on Sunday. Although to this day I can bring back every nuance and feeling of the moment when I learned the news, the rest of that weekend is foggy. I'm not sure why we stayed at my parents' home until Sunday. Maybe we needed to do practical things like wash the dirty clothes from our week's vacation or make phone calls to relatives. There is often so much to *do* in the immediate wake of learning about death.

On Saturday night, after the children were in bed, I said to my mom, "I want to go see a funny movie." She looked at me askance but agreed to drive to a neighborhood theater where *The Odd Couple* was playing.

It was my desperate attempt to *not-know*. If I could sit in the darkness of a theater and hear people laugh at something funny on a colorful screen, then . . . maybe, I thought . . . for two hours . . . I might forget.

Of course, I didn't forget. While Jack Lemmon and Walter Matthau dropped one-liners on each other, I sat in the dark and licked salty tears as they slid down my cheeks into the corners of my mouth.

a helping hand

Grief is sporadic. Your mind fastens on the reality and then veers away just as your eyes veer from direct exposure to the sun. The light is too searing, too intense. You cannot bear it for more than a moment.

When I was twenty-four, and John was still very much alive, I paid my first condolence call on a newly widowed wife of a Navy pilot. I expected to find her prostrate, but to my surprise, she was talking with several other wives about paint chips. They sipped coffee and discussed what color she had planned to paint the family room, almost as if it were an ordinary day. At the time, I was startled—even a little affronted. How could she think of something so trivial when her husband was dead?

After John died, I began to understand.

Turning to God

Going to church after I learned of John's death was like reaching for a life raft in the churning waves. I clung to the familiar prayers of the Catholic Mass and squeezed the hands of my children as we walked together to the communion rail. Our son had celebrated his first communion just a few months before John left for Vietnam. How his dad had beamed. The memory brought tears and a fierce thought: *John would not want to be dead.*

I gasped, barely able to take the consecrated host, and unable to stop the tears. My children looked at me, frightened, not knowing what to do. Hurriedly, my mother bent toward the priest and whispered. Then she took her grandchildren by the hands and walked them to their pew, while I fled the church, giving in to loud sobs as I reached the side yard. The southern California sky was cloudless and blue. Traffic noises sounded in the distance. I leaned against a palm tree, and my prayer became an inarticulate, "Oh God, oh God, oh God."

a helping hand

Whether your prayer is an inarticulate gasp, a solitary walk that connects with nature, or a more ordered religious ceremony, this is a good time to look for spiritual solace. Even if you angrily shake your fist at God, you're acknowledging your need to believe there is more to life than a random existence. Think about the response after the terrorist attack on New York's World Trade Center. People everywhere gathered in churches, mosques, and synagogues for prayer and remembrance. They lit candles, sang hymns, created shrines. It's an instinctive response when serious calamity strikes. As Thomas More said: "Earth has no sorrow that heaven cannot heal."

A Dream Lost

Not every death involves a person. Sometimes your dream may die. When Don was forty-seven, an opportunity came along that he had dreamed of for years—a job as an advertising creative director. So Don moved his wife and teenage sons from Chicago to Kansas City. By the end of the first month, he realized his mistake. The company's owner was a demanding, critical, self-made man who didn't listen to Don's ideas. He merely wanted Don to implement whatever he said to do.

Don was deeply disappointed. He wanted to quit, but how could he uproot his family again? And at his age, how did he know another job would be any better? For a while he foundered. His jaws ached from gritting his teeth.

But prayer was an integral part of Don's life, and through prayer, Don found a creative way to manage his misplaced expectations. He explained it to me this way: "I decided to fire my boss, and work directly for God."

"Oh?" I couldn't help smiling. "And what kind of boss was God?"

Don chuckled. "A good one. I had to do just one thing. Despite my frustrations, I always had to do my best, because God knows if you don't. And that was all I had to do, because God requires no more."

By "working for God" Don found a livable way to say good-bye to his disillusioned job hopes. He couldn't change his circumstances, so he changed the way he interpreted them. Ironically, he showed such grace in handling his critical boss that he became a mentor and role model for many of the company's younger workers.

a helping hand

Say these words: "Just for today, I will adapt to what is." Then add Mahatma Gandhi's statement: "I do the work. I leave the results to God." When Don went to work for God, he put into practice Gandhi's philosophy. It reflects the Buddhist idea that suffering occurs when you cling to *your* idea of what an outcome should be. Certain kinds of losses, especially those that involve frustrated expectations, become more bearable if you can detach yourself from results. Is it easy to do? No. But it's possible.

"Working for God" enabled one man to manage with grace and good-humor what otherwise might have embittered him. Try it. Just for today, adapt to what is.

Loss and Loneliness

Loss doesn't always arrive with a thunderclap. It may come slowly, like seeping water. Many years after John died, I regularly walked for exercise with my friend Marlie. By this time, I was in my fifties, and so was she. I listened as Marlie struggled to decide if she should leave her husband. Her marriage hadn't deteriorated into a battleground. Rather, it was an arid plain. One day she showed me a page from a journal she kept.

"This is my marriage," she said. On the page, she'd written:

> *Lonely.*
> Lonely is
> . . . like a sigh, long and drawn-out, in an empty house,
> . . . like pastel watercolors, faint hues that have no life,
> . . . like walking down an empty street, shuttered houses on either side,
> . . . like calling and calling and hearing only silence.

For years, her successful husband, a busy doctor, had rushed from one appointment to another, too outwardly focused to spend time on his marriage. While the children were growing up, Marlie never thought about leaving. But now the kids were on their own, and their large house echoed with her loneliness.

When she pulled a reluctant Tom into counseling, he expressed bewilderment. He was still Tom; why wasn't that enough? Hadn't he provided well for her?

"And, of course, financially he has," said Marlie, as we circled our walking trail. "But. . . ." Her laugh sounded hollow. "We're like those old married couples you see in restaurants who eat without looking at each other because they have nothing to say." She squeezed my hand. "To be lonely inside of your most intimate relationship is the worst loneliness of all."

a helping hand

Are you lonely? Loneliness can be a wake-up call. It may or may not lead out of a relationship, but it often leads toward change. Loneliness means a sense of separateness, isolation, a lack of intimate connection. If these words resonate, spend some quiet time thinking about your relationships. When do you feel most lonely? Where? With whom? Write down your answers. Follow Marlie's example and write how *lonely* expresses itself to you.

Is it situation specific? The response to a death or the end of a relationship or a geographic move? Are there actions you can take, such as joining a support group, finding a hobby club where people share your interests, or inviting a neighbor for coffee?

Or does your loneliness go deeper, down to the bone? Loneliness may be the cry of your soul, aching to be heard in the clatter of your too-busy life. Befriend your loneliness. Seek to understand it. Let it teach you. If you wish to pray, pray for the wisdom to learn the truth behind your loneliness and for the courage to go wherever that truth takes you.

A Lingering Loss

Earl and Nancy had a warm, loving marriage. When Nancy was terminally ill with cancer, Earl kept a journal.

Nancy's illness is like a long flight of descending stairs. The steps only go down. You try to stay on each step for a time, until the next step down. There's never a hope of climbing up, only going down to the end, which seems to be shadowed and not quite visible.

I want to ask her: Am I doing the right things? Do you have concerns that we haven't discussed? Are you frightened of the days ahead? I know I am. Our communication is very good, yet I feel we're leaving something out that I will someday wish we had discussed.

Our daughter Leslie or I have been with her every minute of the day and night, but still I feel we can't do enough to comfort her or care for her. Other family and friends are caring and kind, too. But this is Nancy we're talking about! Nancy who has always been so strong in will and personality. Nancy who has always known what to do.

I know my pain is nothing compared to hers, but it is real and overpowering at times. I hurt so for her, and I hurt for myself because I don't know what to do. I feel so helpless.

Still, the comfort of our home seems to give her some peace. Out our bedroom window she can see the greenness of trees and grass, the clouds and sky. Is she frightened about her future? I don't think so. She's concerned about her increasing helplessness, but not afraid of the end of her life.

a helping hand

If you're a caregiver, I hope Earl's journal helps you know that your own feelings of helplessness, pain, sorrow, and fear are normal. So, too, are your occasional bursts of hope. I stayed with each of my parents during their terminal illnesses, and as I read Earl's notes, I was struck by the similarity of our feelings, although he was caring for a spouse and I, for a parent. (I wrote about my experience in my book *Nobody's Child Anymore*.) Sometimes we even used identical words. All caregivers share similar emotions and experiences.

Mixed Emotions

On their forty-fifth wedding anniversary, Earl had a florist deliver roses to Nancy. But at 3 p.m. on the same day, he met with the cemetery caretaker to select two burial plots. *"What a chore on your anniversary! Is this really where we will be put in caskets and buried—forever?"*

A short time later, Nancy felt well enough for them to drive to their lake cottage. On their last night at the cottage, Earl wrote: *"I stood on the deck at twilight, and the words from 'Love's Old Sweet Song' kept running through my head: 'Just a song at twilight, when the lights are low, and the drifting shadows seem to come and go.' Driving home, I said I needed to talk 'heavy stuff' for a little and told Nancy about my selection of lots in the old Olathe cemetery. We agreed that there are more scenic places, but they aren't for us. Then Nancy told me she didn't mind if I remarried. 'I won't come back to haunt you,' she said. I told her I would appreciate a haunt. We were both in tears for a little while."*

a helping hand

All losses contain a blend of day-to-day concerns mixed with the sudden knife twist of remembrance. In the first stage of grief, don't be surprised if you're talking about something mundane one minute, and are in tears the next. It's normal. If you're a caregiver, stay alert to your loved one's wishes. Some terminally ill patients want to talk about their impending deaths. Some even plan their own funerals. But others require a certain level of denial. Let your loved one know you are willing to talk, but don't force it.

Finality

Earl's diary continued: *"At 2:30 a.m. it came to a crashing, thundering end—in silence. My daughter Leslie awakened me. 'Dad, come in here. Mom has left us.' I went to Nancy's bedside and saw at once that her half open eyes were without sight or life. I placed my hand on her now cold forehead. 'Oh God, and I wasn't here. I'm sorry, Nancy, I'm so sorry!' I turned to Leslie. 'She's out of it at last.' Leslie replied, 'I know, Dad. She didn't make a sound.' We stood at Nancy's bedside for perhaps five minutes, and the silence was the most intense I have ever felt."*

a helping hand

You may find solace in knowing that the moment of ending often occurs quietly, even gently. I observed that myself when I held, in the span of four years, first, the hand of my father, then my mother, and then my mother-in-law at their moments of death. I saw their faces smooth, heard their breathing lighten, become easy, and then . . . stop.

"The day of death is when two worlds meet with a kiss: this world going out, the future world coming in," wrote the Rabbi Jose ben Abin sixteen hundred years ago.

Not only death, but other losses, too, may bring a moment when two worlds meet—the world going out and the world coming in. It's a moment of still-point, of extraordinary clarity. In that moment, as if lit with brilliant light, you see clearly that what *was* is no more. Especially if you have been engaged in denial, and have ignored the signposts of change, the still-point is somehow welcoming. The human psyche finds strength to deal with reality. It is illusion that damages the soul. After all, isn't reality another name for God?

2.

Unfair Good-Byes

"Father, forgive them,
for they know not what they are doing."

Luke 23:34

No loss is easy, but some seem particularly unfair. Feelings of sadness are mixed with anger and a sense of betrayal. "I did my best. How could this happen to me?" Experts agree: it's harder to say good-bye to a conflicted loss or one that is patently unfair.

You obsess and build pictures in your mind of what you should have said, or should have noticed, or what should be. You heap angry curses on the head of the one who wronged you. You shake your fist at the terrible randomness of life. Sometimes you're angry with yourself. "Why didn't I *see*? How could I have been so stupid that I believed him? Or her?"

Back to the Beginning

Donna and Gary will never forget the day of foreclosure. It was early spring, and still damp and chilly in southeastern Missouri when the family heard wheels on the graveled road leading to their farmhouse. Gary walked to the back window and looked out. The bankers had arrived.

Gary said nothing, just looked toward the little pond and the oak tree, the handmade bird feeders, and the barn where the tractor and other machinery, even their car, was ready for the farm sale.

Their son John, fifteen, who had planned to farm like his dad and granddad and great-granddad, hammered his fist on the table. Tears swam in his eyes. "It's not fair!"

"No, it's not," agreed his mom, and suddenly, Donna ran outside, not even caring that she didn't have a jacket on. She began screaming at the bankers, at the men who were taking away their machinery, their very livelihood.

Gary, Donna, and John were one of many farm families affected by the economic crisis in agriculture. Talking about it later, Donna said, "I want people to know what it's like to lie in bed with a man who feels like a failure. How it feels to live with fear, and the gray fog of 'not knowing.' How ashamed we were to sit next to neighbors in church, knowing we were defaulting on loans. And after years of building a prosperous farm, how it feels to be right back where we started twenty years ago. Maybe it will help others to feel less alone if we share our experience."

a helping hand

It does help to share stories. For Gary and Donna, the particular angst of bankruptcy lay in the fact that it didn't come as a result of poor management or extravagant spending. They were simply caught by economic forces larger than themselves. Their industriousness made no difference.

You, too, may be caught in economic forces beyond your control. Massive corporate lay-offs are common. "Giving up anything you've already secured—anything you have stored away mentally as yours—is a powerful experience whose pain can't be measured in any strict mathematical accounting," wrote Alan Ehrenhalt in *USA Today*.

Many workers feel their loyalty and hard work no longer pay off, so anger is mixed with mourning. The optimistic American culture has always believed you can make something of yourself if you just work hard. To do the work and then discover it makes no difference means you lose more than your job or business. You lose your belief in fair play.

Though it may be hard to remember this at first, you are *more* than your job or your business. In New Testament scripture, Jesus says, "Do not store up for yourselves treasures on earth where moth and rust consume . . . but store up for yourselves treasures in heaven" (Matthew 6:19-20). Your heavenly treasure includes your talent and your inner attitude.

Believe. Believe that you can cope and that you'll move on from this. Look into your past for an example of when you handled a particularly difficult situation. Say aloud several times a day, "*I did it before. I can do it again.*"

Jesus also said, "Blessed are those who mourn, for they will be comforted." It's okay to mourn.

A Terrible Accident

There is also a bewildered rage when something happens that is so bizarre you could never have imagined it. It's as if the underpinnings of life are snatched away.

All Americans experienced this on September 11, 2001. It happened to Anna in June of 1992. She had nothing more serious on her mind than vacation plans as she drove her youngest son Jamie, eleven, home from the dentist. A tractor-trailer rig sped ahead of them on the Pennsylvania highway. Suddenly, the eighteen-wheeler rolled over a large chunk of concrete that was loose on the highway. The truck's wheels acted like a slingshot and sent a fifty-pound boulder hurtling toward their windshield.

"Mom!" yelled Jamie, seeing it first. Anna raised her left arm in a futile gesture as the boulder smashed directly into her face and head. She slumped, unconscious. Blood, glass, bone, and twisted metal spewed everywhere. Jamie managed to grab the wheel and brake on the highway shoulder. He saved their lives.

The bones in Anna's face were smashed like pieces of crushed eggshell. Her eyesight was destroyed. Miraculously, she had no long-term brain injury, but steel plates had to be inserted in her head. One side of her face was paralyzed, and she lost all her teeth. Small children sometimes screamed in fright when they first saw her.

Who would expect that on a simple car trip to the dentist a boulder would crash through your front windshield and destroy your face and eyesight?

Who among the passengers on September 11, 2001, expected their plane to become a deadly missile?

a helping hand

Everyone feels a secret fear that maybe life *is* random. When events make no sense, it's crucial to find comfort in something that gives your world meaning again.

To quickly satisfy yourself that God is real, take these four steps, advises Tom Powers, in his book *Invitation to a Great Experiment.*

◆ "First, accept God as a working hypothesis. Sincerely ask him, if he exists, to help you and steer you.

◆ "Second, find and associate with a group of people who really do believe in God and who are working their belief in daily life.

◆ "Third, be open and truthful with these people about your situation and follow the reasonable suggestions they make to you.

◆ "Fourth, keep an open mind and watch. The evidence of God's presence and influence will appear in your own life, possibly sooner than you expect."

Anna found her evidence of God several months after her accident. She sat alone in the convalescent center, weeping. Suddenly she cried aloud, "Where are you, God? I'm hurting. I'm alone. *Please*, help me." Despite her blindness, she seemed to see a door open. A bright light appeared, and she heard the words, as clearly as if a voice had spoken: "It will be all right."

"From that day forward, in spite of the pain and darkness, I knew I would manage," said Anna.

Stay alert. Practice the four steps above, and look for grace as it appears in your life.

Unaccepted

To be spurned because of your very nature—the part of you that can't be changed—seems like the ultimate unfair loss. It happened to Jason, and I'd like to share his story in his own words.

I knew I was different as far back as I can remember, back when I was five years old, although I didn't have words for it. In fifth grade, I finally understood I had a different sexual orientation.

My parents split up when I was seven and I lived with my mom. I thought we had a wonderful relationship. When I was a high school junior, though, I got tired of not being honest, so I sat down beside her one night and asked, "Mom, would you love me no matter what?"

My mom is tiny, just over five feet tall, and pretty. She got a scared look on her face. "Mom, I'm gay."

She didn't say a word, just got up, went into her bathroom, and threw up.

"Mom, it's nothing I'm doing to you. It's just who I am. I want us to be honest with each other."

She walked out of the bathroom, stiff legged, down to the kitchen, and I heard glass shatter. Like bombs exploding. She threw every glass in the cupboard at the wall. The next day she sent me to a psychiatrist. Actually, I was glad to go. I needed to talk to someone. After one visit, the psychiatrist told my mother I was mature, healthy, and homosexual, and she should accept and love me.

Instead, she ripped and broke most of our furniture, dishes, and clothes. She started slapping me and raking her fingernails across my face. Then she threw herself down and wailed. It was such an eerie sound.

"Mom," I pleaded, "What can I do? What can I say?"
She looked up with this—this crazy look on her face.

"You cannot—you will not—" she gasped, and start-
ed scratching her own face, making it bleed.

I got so scared, I called my aunt Marge, my father's
sister, and went to stay with her and her husband Bill,
who's a sociology professor. I was too scared to say the
words "I'm gay" to them, but I took along some poetry I'd
written and showed it to Uncle Bill. He read it and said,
"Jason, are you gay?" I nodded and he hugged me. So did
Aunt Marge.

I lived with them the rest of my junior year because
Mom kept threatening to send me to Europe to get "fixed."

When I told my dad, he felt guilty because he thought
he'd caused it by being an absentee father. But over and
over, I told him I always felt different, even before the
divorce. We got really close after that. My dad asked me to
live with him my senior year.

My mother has never accepted me. I realize now she
doesn't know how to really love me. She only loved her per-
ception—her fantasy—of who I should be. When I didn't
fulfill her dream, she shut me out.

But I still miss her.

a helping hand

When you're rejected for being yourself, there's
an awful pain, especially if the rejection comes from
the person who means the most to you. It may make
you feel ashamed, or so desperate to find acceptance,
you will try to be other than who you are. But that
choice leads you away from spiritual wholeness and
joy. Whether stated in psychological or religious
terms, everyone's life task is to "know thyself."

It's hard to acknowledge that you're not loved.
Love, as it's so well defined by M. Scott Peck in
The Road Less Traveled, is when one chooses to extend

oneself for one's own spiritual growth or another's. To grow spiritually, you must be allowed to be authentically who you are.

If the person you love most is unable to love you for who you are or to care about your spiritual growth, then at some point you must find the courage to mentally say good-bye to that person. The serenity prayer captures it well: *"God, grant me the serenity to accept the things I cannot change, courage to change the things I can, and the wisdom to know the difference."*

'Til Death Do Us Part

I once saw a *New Yorker* cartoon that showed a couple at the altar. The minister was saying, "Do you promise to love and cherish until death or diverging careers do you part?" When I saw it, I chuckled, but also, I felt sad as I thought of all the Hollywood couples whose careers seemed to end their marriages.

The rest of us—and perhaps, most star couples, too—marry with the idea that we will "love and cherish, 'til death do us part." When the one you love leaves you, it's a terrible blow.

Mary Ann had been married for sixteen years when her husband told her he loved another woman and wanted a divorce. The couple had four children, all enrolled in parochial schools. Mary Ann had been a young bride—barely eighteen—and to her, marriage was for life. Now, as her picture-perfect world shattered, a voice cried in her head, *How could God let this happen?*

Day after day for the next six months, she sat sobbing on the living room sofa. Even though she later admitted to herself that at some level she had suspected his love affair, Mary Ann never thought her husband would leave her. "It hurt so much," she recalled. "Everything I believed in had disappeared." Bitterness seemed to invade her very bones.

One day her grandmother appeared at her door. She been deserted by her husband too, but had managed to work and raise her son successfully. In her practical, no-nonsense voice, she declared, "You've cried long enough, Mary Ann. Get up! You've got to get going for your children's sake. If you don't make it, they won't make it."

Her grandmother looked so fierce that Mary Ann found herself laughing—shakily—through her tears. Obediently, she stood up. "Good," said her grandmother. She gave her granddaughter a hug. "God helps those who help themselves."

a helping hand

Betrayal by someone you trust is like an earthquake. The very ground beneath you is suddenly unstable. You may decide, "I have been wronged. I deserve to feel angry and bitter." And who would dispute you?

Bitterness, though, is like a boomerang. You send it soaring out toward the person or situation that has wronged you, and it comes back. You're the one who is hurt.

At the National Institute of Healthcare Research, Michael McCullough, Ph.D. developed a program of empathy training to help people change their way of thinking about their betrayal. Empathy helps you *reframe* your hurt by finding a cause for the offense that is independent of a desire to hurt you. There are four steps.

1. Begin by thinking about times *you* have hurt others. Were you deliberately trying to hurt?

2. Recall when you have been forgiven. How did you
feel when you needed someone's forgiveness?

3. Visualize your aggressor's state of mind and
explain the hurtful event from the aggressor's
viewpoint.

4. See if you can go beyond the event itself to feel
the frailty and humanness of the person who hurt
you.

Isn't the same advice contained in the New
Testament? "First take the log out of your own eye,
and then you will see clearly to take the speck out of
your neighbor's eye" (Matthew 7:5).

Other Betrayals

Betrayal can occur in many ways and in many
relationships—between business partners, between
friends, in parent-child relationships, between sib-
lings. When Carla and Hazel's widowed mother
died, the two sisters inherited her modest estate,
divided equally between them. Carla, the elder and
more conservative, put hers in the bank. "College
funds for Hank," she said, referring to her son.

Hazel, four years younger and single, grinned
and spun her sister around. "I'm going to be a
dot.com millionaire, sis. You watch. I'm using my
money to start an Internet business."

Hazel was adept with computers and her business took off. But as the 1990s ended, problems
emerged, and Hazel went to see her sister. "I've got a
big investor waiting in the wings, but it's taking
longer than I thought to close the deal. Can you help
me, sis? Your money will be safe. This is just a tem-
porary cash flow problem." She flashed her usual
grin. "If you like, I'll sell you shares and make *you* a
dot.com millionaire."

Carla hesitated. She was counting on her portion of the estate to pay her son's tuition in September. Still, here was Hazel, holding out a carefully written business plan, and looking her straight in the eye, and Carla, the big sister, had always tried to help her younger sister.

So she transferred her funds. But she asked Hazel to treat it as a loan. "I don't need to be a millionaire," said Carla. "I just want the money back for Hank's tuition." When September approached without repayment, Carla called her sister. Hazel put her off. A month passed. Then Hazel showed up at her sister's door. Her mascara was streaked. She'd been crying. "Oh God, Carla, I'm sorry. So sorry!"

Hazel had lost all the money. The investor had disappeared. She was declaring bankruptcy.

As Carla told me the story, she, too, started weeping.

"She knew how important that money was to Hank, and she knew I'm a pushover when it comes to helping family. We haven't spoken in two years. I still feel so betrayed! But I miss my sister too."

a helping hand

Forgiveness does not deny what has happened. It's a willingness to search for a truth that lies beyond the situation. If you find yourself in a situation similar to Carla's, ask yourself if you acted in the role of *rescuer*. Despite her intuitive desire to say no, Carla allowed herself to be manipulated by her sister into playing that role.

Now she feels torn between her sense of betrayal and her love for her sister. Dr. McCullough's research showed that people attribute others' misbehavior to malice, while seeing their own misdeeds as the result of passing circumstance. Actually, everyone's motives are mixed.

An excellent resource for changing rescuer behavior is Harriet Lerner's book *The Dance of Anger*.

And don't forget prayer.

If you want to forgive and are finding it hard, turn to Psalm 23. Say the words slowly, substituting plural pronouns for singular. "The Lord is *our* shepherd, *we* shall not want." Read it aloud each day for nine days. It will help you to see youself and your betrayer as connected in the family of God. "He leads us *both* beside still waters. He restores both our souls."

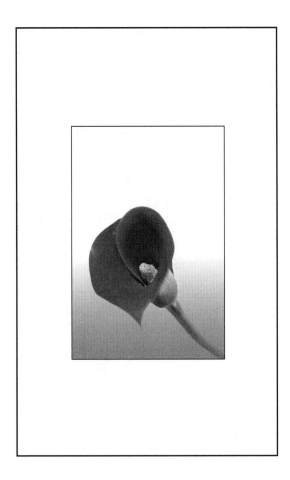

3.

Saying Good-Bye to Lost Expectations

*Oft expectation fails and most oft
there where most it promises.*

William Shakespeare

The decades of young adulthood—our twenties and thirties—are generally times of acquiring. We acquire an education, a job, a car, possibly a spouse, a house, and a child (often in that order). We buy furniture, stereos, and computers. In our adding years, we don't expect something precious to be taken away. A loss hits particularly hard because it's out of sync with our expectations.

Even though my husband John was a Navy fighter pilot and even though I knew it was a risky profession, I absolutely, positively believed that if I were a reasonably good person, John and my children would be safe. It was my bargain with God.

For years after John died, one feeling that stayed with me was a sense of wide-eyed *surprise*. As life unfolded in ways I hadn't expected, part of me kept murmuring, "But this isn't what my life was supposed to be like!" It was as if my expected life were a room, with all its furniture arranged just so. Then a hurricane came along and knocked the furniture askew. New pieces and new colors were added, but it wasn't the original room, and I wasn't sure how I felt about that.

Everyone carries into adulthood an unspoken bargain with God—or Life—and at some point will cry, "This isn't what I expected!" Part of growing up (versus merely growing older) is relinquishing our own ideas, our bargains with God, and finding instead a way to grow in whatever comes into our lives.

Kidding Ourselves

Five years after John died, I remarried. By then, I'd adopted an independent stance as a career woman and the head of my family. The women's movement was at its height, and Bill and I solemnly professed our mutual belief in an egalitarian marriage.

I chuckle now as I recall the contract we designed. We thought it would head off any problems. We were so specific! Under *Money*, we agreed that each of us would contribute equally. Under *Cooking*, each of us would cook three nights of the week with Sundays reserved for dinners out. Under *Children*, Bill would act as a father to my children, and I would be a friend to his slightly older three.

We were so proud of our contract!

But two weeks before we married, Bill lost his job, and I became the sole income producer. To my annoyance, Bill found excuses for not cooking. And his tough-minded views on child-rearing were totally opposite mine. Before long, our careful contractual arrangements had flown out the window.

In the beginning, Bill said he liked the way I quickly expressed my feelings. "Nothing stays hidden," he said.

Except that *everything* was hidden, even from ourselves. For all our liberated talk, we'd grown up in the fifties, and each of us brought baggage from that era. I didn't want to be the sole financial provider. Bill didn't want to do housework and cooking. After losing his job, he borrowed money and launched his own business. When the business didn't take off, I grew resentful and he became defensive. Our different attitudes toward raising children added to the stress.

One day my anger boiled over. Burning words spilled out, stinging Bill for not contributing financially. Bill responded by berating my parenting skills. "If it weren't for me, the kids would be out of control!" he snapped.

Each of us knew the other's soft spots. Eventually we both said we were sorry, and moved on, but the same issues came up again. And again. For years, our marriage was like a circular dance. All that really changed was the intensity of our arguments. Eventually, nothing was left but blame, guilt, and a kind of rage because nothing had turned out as we had expected.

a helping hand

Are you caught up in repetitive fighting with your spouse or one of your kids or your own parent? In *The Dance of Anger*, author Harriet Lerner explains that when people get stuck in ineffective fighting, they're usually trying to change the other, but are afraid or unwilling to change themselves. By repeating the same old fights, you're releasing anger yet protecting yourself from the anxieties attached to real change.

It requires courage to stop playing the "if only" game (If only he/she would change, everything would be fine) and take responsibility for your own choices. It means stepping out of the illusion that your partner or another "should" be a certain kind of person or that your relationship "should" follow certain expectations.

Become clear in your own mind about what is happening in your relationship. If there's a lot of anger, realize that anger usually covers up two more basic emotions: sadness or fear. Why are you sad? What do you fear?

Subconsciously, you could be afraid that if you take responsibility for real change, it could end your relationship. But as Bill and I sadly learned, problems do not go away. Losing a relationship is painful, but even more painful is the circular path of repeated anger. Sometimes it's necessary to simply let go.

Finality

"At least death is a clean slice of the knife. Divorce is a hacking away," said Maura. We sat at one of the tables outside the college student union where both of us attended grad school. Maura was going through a divorce while I was still grieving over John's death.

I remembered what Maura had said as I faced my second husband in a divorce lawyer's office twenty-five years later. I looked—almost in wonder—at the man whom for twenty years I had slept with and shared a bathroom with; whose mother had died holding my hand. His hair was almost gone now and his face was grizzled. But what I noticed most were his eyes. They stared at me so coldly across the conference table. Who was this stranger? How had we arrived at such a place?

Bill had accused me of taking his Beethoven CD. That's what we fought over at the end. Two voices screaming at each other, as Bill yelled and I protested, then capitulated, "All right, if you think I took it, I'll buy you another one!" But it wasn't about the CD, of course.

Is the breakdown of a relationship ever about just one thing?

In a kind of frenzied distress during our final argument, I grabbed my Bible and began to frantically pull out pages of the Old Testament. It was as if I symbolically needed to show that the old contract—our marriage contract—was ripped beyond repair. Bill knew how much my Bible meant to me, and my actions stopped him cold. Wordless, we simply looked at one another.

Now, inside the lawyer's office, no one spoke as we signed papers. Bill left first. Then I walked, alone, into the late September sunshine. Around me, autumn leaves were starting to turn, and I felt a peculiar giddiness. I was sad—yet relieved. A weight seemed to have lifted.

Our marriage was dead. We had publicly acknowledged a truth that for too long I had not wanted to face. Did a new beginning lie in my future? And in his? Would there first be more hacking away?

a helping hand

People who haven't gone through divorce seldom appreciate the wild mix of feelings in what author Abigail Trafford calls "crazy time."

You do feel crazy for a while. Numbed and enraged. Shocked and bewildered. Relieved yet angry. Angry at your spouse. Angry at yourself. "How did this happen? Why couldn't we make it work? How can he/she reject me like this?"

As one counselor said with a kind of black humor, whether you are the Dumper or the Dumpee, the act of taking apart a relationship is extraordinarily painful. You feel tattered and bruised; truly, it is like being hacksawed. In some ways, I found divorce more painful than death.

It hurts to say good-bye to the dream you shared when you promised to "love and cherish from this day forward." And if your family or religious heritage stressed the idea that marriage lasts "until death do us part," you may feel an added weight of shame and failure.

As with any death, you must mourn the passing of your marriage, and that takes time. Unlike death, divorce has no funeral—with its public show of support—so it's up to you to let friends and family know you need them to be there for you.

In the early time of separation, when you feel so bloodied, hold on to a belief that "this too shall pass." One day you *will* feel better. One day you will pass out of this shadowed valley.

Fr. Thomas Keating, a Trappist monk known for his writings on centering prayer, said in a homily I heard: "God is present in every circumstance." Even, he continued, when you think or act as if God is absent.

No Wizard

Not long after we separated, I had a dream in which I was Dorothy walking down the yellow brick road of Oz. As I reached the Emerald City, I found the wizard (who bore an amazing resemblance to my ex-husband). Just as in the actual story, my little dog pulled up the curtain and revealed the wizard as a sham—a humbug. He wasn't who he said he was. "Oh, you are a very bad man!" I cried. But in my dream, just as in the story, he replied: "No, I'm a good man. I'm just a very bad wizard."

I woke up sweating, not wanting to admit what the dream was forcing me to see: I had wanted Bill to be my wizard—someone strong, protective, and financially successful—and when he didn't meet my expectations, I had felt disappointed and resentful.

Part of me wanted to point an angry finger. It's always tempting to accuse and blame an ex-spouse. But deep within, another part of me recognized that Bill wasn't a *bad* man, no more than I was a bad woman. He was just a flawed, imperfect human being who—like me—had made mistakes. It didn't mean our marriage could be salvaged, for we had long since passed that possibility, but it did mean I had to stop looking for a wizard to save me. Like Dorothy, it was time to take my own journey.

a helping hand

Divorce is a time of uncertainty and letting go, but it can also be the start of exciting self-discovery. A willingness to recognize the humanness of your

former spouse—to acknowledge that no one is a wizard and seldom is anyone a complete ogre—doesn't
mean you won't feel angry, hurt, betrayed, bereft; all
the mad-sad-glad feelings that make divorce such an
emotional roller coaster. It does mean you commit
yourself to learning rather than blaming. There's a
vital difference between accurately acknowledging
responsibility and playing the blame/guilt game.

Prayer can be very important during divorce,
because it brings you the grace to avoid bitterness
and work toward a state of forgiveness. Consider this
petition, which I wrote in my own prayer journal:
"Oh God, help me believe in myself. Help me work
and live without comparing. Give me the persever-
ance to discover myself and all that I can be."

No Promotion

Marriage is only one arena where people can hold
false expectations. Work is another.

Sonya was my neighbor when I first moved to
Kansas City, and even though we now live in different neighborhoods, we've remained friends. She
went to work for a government agency straight out of
college, and has worked there for twenty-three years.
Last year, she was passed over for an expected
promotion. To make matters worse, a younger, less
experienced colleague did get promoted.

Sonya felt humiliated. Telling me about it later,
she said, "I went to work the next day knowing that
people were speculating about me. What had I done
wrong—or failed to do?"

When she asked her department director why, he
was noncommittal.

"I guess I'm not politically correct," she said
bitterly.

Sonya found it harder and harder to drag herself out of bed in the mornings, and although she completed her work assignments, she stopped speaking up in departmental meetings and began eating lunch alone at her desk.

"I'd love to quit," she said, "but I can't afford to leave. I'm too close to retirement. And I need the benefits."

Feeling dead-ended in a job can be like a Chinese water-torture. Your satisfaction and self-confidence erode drop by drop.

a helping hand

When you're twenty-one, it's easy to picture yourself becoming president. But realistically, there isn't room at the top for everyone. And are you sure you *want* to be president? Author Stephen Covey says it's possible to climb to the top of a ladder and then realize you leaned your ladder against the wrong building.

If your job is at a plateau, or you lose a hoped-for promotion, or perhaps a hoped-for new job, acknowledge it. Your pain is legitimate. But if you can't move up, can you see yourself moving sideways? Are there ways to enrich the job you have or move laterally within your organization?

A plateau may leave you more time to pursue other things that matter in your life. Psychiatrist Viktor Frankl, a Jewish Holocaust survivor, wrote that no one can take away your final freedom—the freedom you have to choose your response to any situation. Perhaps now is the time to broaden your definition of success. Spend some quiet time thinking about your life beyond your job. Remember the quip,

"On their death bed, no one wishes they'd spent more time at the office." What does real success mean?

Too Many Birthdays

Dottie's younger friend Lauren said to her, as they swam at Dottie's pool, "We've got to plan something wonderful for three years from now—a trip to Paris or at least New York."

"Why? What's happening three years from now?"

"It's your birthday. You'll be seventy!"

Dottie, who had been languidly floating on a rubber raft, was so startled, she fell into the water and came up sputtering. Later, she said to me, "I hated being reminded that I'm just three years short of seventy!"

"It's like the first time the supermarket checker calls you ma'am," I said.

"Or worse: when the checkout guy doesn't even *see* you," added Dottie.

It seems like a small thing, really, the awareness of lost youth. Yet as the years pile up, the inevitable reminders are there—in stiffened knees, changes in body shape, color of hair, hearing loss. The idea of getting old is still anathema to most people.

Even my friend Pat, who weighs the same at sixty as she did at twenty (and this, after birthing five babies), admits that her body has shifted in some inevitable post-menopausal way.

I once spoke to an eighty-eight-year-old woman who was too ill to get out of bed. Her hand, clasping mine, felt like tissue paper. "But honey, inside this decrepit body, I'm still sixteen," she insisted.

"Autumn" can be a poignant time of life. You start every day with a handful of pills. You pick up

Depends at the drugstore. You read obituaries and notice when someone died who is younger than you. Days and months seem to hurtle past, until you realize, with surprise, that another year is already gone. To say good-bye to youth and accept our own aging is one of the hardest things most of us will do.

a helping hand

"Years wrinkle the skin but to give up enthusiasm wrinkles the soul," wrote Samuel Ullman. The older person who measures "high" in life satisfaction is someone who retains enthusiasm for life *as it is*, and who discovers a way of living that incorporates a higher meaning—a meaning in terms you consider important.

Whether you replace lost relationships and activities with vigorous new ones, or focus more deeply on just one or two interests, or choose a quieter life of inner contemplation, you'll live enthusiastically once you say good-bye to regretful yearnings to be twenty again.

The great psychologist Carl Jung divided life into halves. The first half, he said, is when you form your ego and establish yourself in the world. The second half is when you find a larger meaning for all that effort.

Sure, your knees creak, but embrace what this stage of life holds. Now is the time for you to decide what gives your life its meaning.

4.

Mixed Good-Byes

It is a painful thing to look at your own trouble and know that you yourself and no one else has made it.

Sophocles

Any loss hurts, but if yours results from something you did or a decision you made, grief is compounded. Guilt may haunt you and become a burden you carry like a weight on your shoulders. Or perhaps you feel you don't deserve to grieve, that your loss isn't important enough, or that you're a survivor when others were not, and you should be grateful, not sad. How do you move forward when your heart is filled with such mixed feelings?

All My Fault

Terrie was driving only a mile down a quiet road, going from her sister's house to her own, so she didn't worry when her four-year-old son Joey scrambled into the back seat and didn't buckle up. They were going such a short distance.

She began backing out of her sister's driveway, her door not yet shut. The sudden movement caused Joey to lose his balance. He fell forward, tangled his head in her driver's shoulder harness, and pitched through the still-open car door. The harness tightened. Terrie jammed her foot on the brake, but Joey's face had already turned blue from the noose of the shoulder harness. As Terrie screamed, "I killed my son!" relatives ran from the house and untangled Joey. They rushed him to the hospital.

X-rays showed a horrifying reality. Joey's spine had been wrenched completely away from his skull. Groundbreaking surgery saved Joey's life, but he was left disabled. Terrie is still haunted by her failure to seat-belt her son.

It is one of a parent's or grandparent's worst nightmares: that you could have prevented the accident that harmed the child in your care.

a helping hand

The hardest person to forgive is yourself. If it seems impossible to do, remember that God forgives everyone, over and over, so for you to refuse yourself forgiveness is to set yourself above God.

True forgiveness, though, includes repentance, a word that means to change and go in a new direction. You can't shift directions until you see clearly and honestly where you are. To repent, you must acknowledge reality, which means looking without blinders at what you did, and any harm it caused, whether intentional or unintentional. Face yourself squarely and acknowledge your responsibility. Say good-bye to denial and rationalization. Decide what reparation you must make and what behavior may need to change. And release expectations that you are perfect and can never make mistakes.

Two strong affirmations are these: *"I am responsible for my choices,"* and *"Everybody is doing the best they can."*

Fatherless Children

After John died, I felt such sorrow for my fatherless children. I made a vow to follow our family practice and take them on weekend outings. In the first months, we explored museums, visited skating rinks, and spread our towels on nearly every beach in San Diego.

What I didn't realize was this: while their daddy was alive, ours was a family that had fun together. Love was carried on wings of laughter. But John had been the catalyst. Now, I had no laughter left in me. I took the children places, but more like a chaperone than a parent. At the skating rink, I sat on the sidelines while the kids skated. At the beaches, while they splashed in the surf, I sat on my towel and read—or stared, blindly, at the rolling ocean, yearning for John and all that I had lost.

I was there . . . yet I wasn't there.

What my daughter Allison remembers about that time is how often I shut my bedroom door and left the children to eat dinner alone, in a puddle of dim light from the TV set.

I was present in our home . . . yet I wasn't.

Most nights, I lay across my bed and grieved, feeling like a rudderless boat about to capsize from the waves that engulfed me.

a helping hand

"For a period of time, your children lost two parents, not just one, when their father died," said a counselor. It can be true in divorce as well. An Ohio State University study found that many parents report diminished parenting practices immediately following divorce. Despite your best intentions, as you struggle to handle your own emotions, your ability to nurture and be there for your child may momentarily lessen. This is a good time to ask for help from any family members who live nearby. Or seek out a particularly good friend. Ask if they'll spend some quality time with your children. Then speak frankly to your kids. Tell them you love them and that you're having a hard time right now. Make it very clear that if they feel they're not getting the attention from you that they would like, it's not about them. It's only your own sadness. Ask them to tell you if they need more. And if everything seems suddenly to start caving in on you, seek professional help. It's often through others that God's grace acts in our lives.

Grief Expressions

My three children each responded differently to their father's death.

John, my seven-year-old, didn't seem to grieve at all. I felt annoyed—angry even—that I hadn't seen him cry. If anything, he stayed outdoors roughhousing with the neighborhood boys even more than usual.

One day I found him playing with his friend Jimmy. John had picked up one of his father's model airplanes. He zoomed the airplane over his head, making noises. Suddenly, with a rumbly, "v-rooom-pow!" he made the airplane dive. It crashed into the family room couch, and he laughed hysterically.

I stood in the doorway. A cold tingle ran through me, followed by a flash of burning heat that rose through my fingers, into my cheeks.

"How dare you laugh!" I shouted. "Your father died in a plane crash. Don't you care? Don't you care that your father is *dead*?"

The laughter stopped, like water turned off. The boys stared at me, at my upraised arm, at the wild look in my eyes. Jimmy seemed uncertain, embarrassed, but oh, the stricken look on John's face! His eyes grew enormous, the pupils black and dilated, and his mouth worked, as if he wanted to speak, but nothing came out. My anger left as suddenly as it had come.

"John," I whispered. "I'm sorry."

But he didn't seem to hear. He simply stood by the couch, one hand still touching the fallen jet airplane. Jimmy sidled past me and ran out our front door. I took a step toward John, but he pushed past me and ran out after Jimmy.

I stood alone in the family room, ashamed of my behavior. I had no experience with childhood grief, and didn't understand it. I didn't realize that grief can be buried, or how destructive such buried grief can be. Of all my three children, John was the child in greatest peril.

a helping hand

Today, many books and support systems exist to help people deal with grief. That wasn't so thirty

years ago, and eventually I had to forgive myself—
and ask my children's forgiveness—for the way I
failed to meet their needs after their daddy died.
Although my mistakes were borne of ignorance and
my own feelings of loss, they were still damaging,
especially to my son John.

Never think that because someone doesn't mourn
in an obvious way that the grief is any less. It may
even be more, and unexpressed grief may emerge
later in more destructive ways—as anger or bodily
ailments.

Take advantage of the many available sources
today—starting with the web—that can help you
understand your own and others' grief.

All Gone!

The terrible irony of it. That's what Marcie thought
later. They'd gone to midnight Mass, then risen early
so the kids could see what Santa brought. A big
Southern breakfast, more gifts to unwrap, afternoon
visits by aunts and uncles and Grandma. Turkey dinner. Pecan pie. No snow in Biloxi, Mississippi—but
holiday lights on the boats in the bay. Everyone
agreed, "What a good Christmas!"

By nine o'clock on Christmas night, even the kids
were tuckered out, and the whole family went to bed.
It was a little past midnight—Marcie noticed because
the figures 12:07 glowed on their bedside alarm
clock. Brad was shaking her shoulders. "Wake up. I
smell smoke." She smelled it too. And instantly came
awake. It smelled sooty, like a fireplace with a
buildup of ashes. And rancid, as if plastics were
burning.

By now, barefoot, in her nightgown, she was running down the hall, yelling at the kids, "Get up! Get
up!" Throwing open bedroom doors. One thought in

her mind: *Kids. Out. Safe.* Brad behind her, carrying Lillie, their youngest, herding them all downstairs. A siren's wail in the distance mixed with Lillie's screams. *Who called the fire department?* wondered Marcie. It seemed an idle thought because only one thing really mattered: *Kids. Out. Safe.* Everyone running out the back door. Running across the grass, barefoot. It was cold. Even near the Gulf, it got cold in December.

Lights flickered on in other houses. Then—*Oh thank God.* Marcie stopped. Counted heads. Everyone, even the dog, was safe. And just in time. Flames leaped through the roof. Licked the night sky. A fire engine screeched to a stop at the curb. Firefighters in dark coats were jumping out, grabbing hoses. "Ma'am, move back please." More flames. It looked like a bonfire. But it was their house. They had saved six years for the down payment. Everything they owned was in it. All the Christmas gifts! The family photos! But—Marcie pulled the children close. *We're alive. That's what counts. Thank you, God.*

Brad's arm went around her. His voice was soft, sad. "I don't think they'll save it, Marcie. I think it's gone."

He was right. By morning, their house had burned to the ground. For weeks afterward, she would start to say, "Oh, I'll get the—" and then stop, realizing. *It's gone. Everything. Gone.*

Insurance replaced some of it. But none of the really important things. The family heirlooms. The kids' photos. The letter Brad had written her on their tenth anniversary. And yet. . . .

"We're safe. We're alive. Thank God. We have what's important," said Marcie. She said it over and over to her shocked family and friends. She meant it. It was true. At the same time, she felt so sad.

Everything! Gone! Even our toothbrushes! She couldn't help it. She wept.

a helping hand

The extraordinary gift of being alive! Sometimes it takes a near death experience to restore the wonder of the gift. If your life is saved, is it shameful, then, to grieve lost possessions? Doesn't scripture say, "Where a your treasure is, there your heart will be also"? (Matthew 6:21).

Some possessions, like a TV, a sofa, or kitchen pots and pans, can be replaced. But other beloved artifacts are irreplaceable, and in these you store memories and pass on family history. Of course you grieve their loss.

Many circumstances prompt the loss of meaningful personal possessions. Your mother may have to give up hers when she moves into a nursing home. Your home could be in the path of a major flood or a tornado. You could return from vacation to learn vandals broke in to smash and destroy.

Don't feel ashamed of your grief if you lose the important memorabilia of your life. You need to say good-bye and acknowledge your loss in the same way you do when a person dies. The quantity of grief may pale next to the loss of a loved one, but the stages and the feelings are just as real.

When Babies Die

"You can't know what it's like to try so hard for a baby until you've been there," said Laurie. She and her husband Don, both in their thirties, had spent two years trying to have a child. Finally, eight months after her first visit to a fertility clinic, Laurie learned she was pregnant. And with twins!

The babies weren't due until April, but when good friends stopped by on December 21 to leave stuffed teddy bears for the twins, Laurie was thrilled. *Our babies' first Christmas gifts!* she thought. She was twenty-four weeks pregnant.

The next day she noticed some spotting and felt a few cramps, but went to work anyway. By nightfall, her cramps had worsened, so Laurie's doctor checked her into the hospital.

At 12:30 a.m., a sudden deep contraction made Laurie cry out. Baby Thomas was born on December 23 weighing one pound, four ounces. Three hours later, Robert was born. He had severe abnormalities.

As other families prepared for Christmas, Laurie and Don hovered between their babies' hospital cribs. By December 24, baby Robert's heart had stopped three times and been restarted. Tears rolled down Laurie's cheeks when the neonatal specialist said quietly, "I'm sorry. I can't save your son." On New Year's Eve, the red-numbered setting on Thomas' ventilator jumped to thirty: it was the point of no return. Laurie put her head down and wept. "No! How can we lose both?" she cried.

a helping hand

Despite her doctors' assurances that it wasn't her fault, Laurie felt tormented by "shoulds." "*I should have quit work. I should have stayed home. I should never have gotten up to use the bathroom in the hospital.*" In her journal, she wrote, "My job was to take care of our babies until they could survive on their own, and I failed. Oh, I hope Don isn't blaming me. Do I dare get pregnant again?"

The pain of losing a child is not lessened because the child is an infant or born with physical infirmities. Anyone who mistakenly thinks, "You didn't have your child for very long, so you won't be as sad," is very wrong. There is intense bonding even before a child is born.

The loss of an infant is also the loss of all-that-might-have-been—all the talents and giggles, all the love and joy—that comes when you watch your child grow up. It hurts a grieving parent to hear a well-meaning friend say, "God must have needed another angel in heaven," because such Pollyanna sympathy seems to ignore the powerful, legitimate sorrow.

If your soul carries an added burden of unnecessary guilt, it is hard to hear the truth when others say, "It's not your fault," or, "You did all you could." One of the most effective resources is a support group where you can share your feelings with others who have had similar experiences. Today, such groups even exist on the web. Don't try to heal alone. And don't try to heal without God, even if your prayer is an inarticulate cry, "Please, God, help me. I hurt so much!"

Missing!

On the night of their daughter's high school graduation, Janis and Stuart McCall said an easy "Yes" when she asked to spend the night with her best friend. For years, the two girls had taken turns spending nights at each other's houses.

But something terrible happened that night, and ten long years later, the McCalls still don't know what. The two girls, along with the girlfriend's mother, disappeared! They have never been seen again. The police surmise abduction, but have been unable to solve the case.

The McCalls live in a nice neighborhood in a small, friendly Midwestern city. *How could such a thing happen here?* Even after ten years, Janis's voice expresses her disbelief. *Not to us! Surely not to us!*

"Not knowing what happened to our daughter is even worse than death," said Janis, "because you can never start your mourning. There is always the hope she might be alive." Her voice caught. A few months ago, on a vacation to Mexico—the first vacation she and her husband had taken in years—Janis found herself looking at every tourist face because maybe, just maybe, one would be her daughter.

Stuart's faith in God was shaken. "I tell Stu that it wasn't God who took our daughter, it was some awful human being," said Janis, "but he says he doesn't know why God allowed it to happen, especially since Stu felt he was a good and faithful servant." A pause. "Somewhere inside, I think Stu still knows there is God. He just doesn't know how to get in touch with him."

The McCalls have tried to move on, but something hangs in the wind, rustling in their memories, twisting in their hearts. Is their daughter dead? Or possibly alive? Oh God, if only they could know!

a helping hand

As painful as it is to say good-bye, be grateful if your circumstances allow you to *know* what happened. The unknown is the hardest of all to bear. It's a landscape wrapped in fog.

What if you don't know the outcome of a loss? What if it's not a child, thank God, but your beloved pet that disappears and is never found? What if you're fired, not merely let go, and no one tells you why? What if a friend stops seeing you and won't answer calls or tell you what happened? What if your soldier husband is missing in action and thought to be dead, but no bodily remains are ever found?

You live with a hole in your heart, a question mark in your soul. But at some point, as one grieving parent said, "You make a decision to stay sane and go on living." Be kind to yourself as you mourn, and allow the process to take as long as it takes. Slowly reconstruct your life. In some cases, for instance, if a friend has dropped from sight, think back. Did you miss some early signals of trouble? Be gentle with yourself as you ask questions.

Janis and Stuart turned their grief into something positive by creating a web site, *OneMissingLink.com*, which offers help to other families who have a child who has disappeared. You may want to do something or contribute to a good cause in your missing beloved's name.

Prayer seems crucial in such circumstances. In such pain, where else can one turn but God? It is a God without answers, a God about whom the poet Rilke wrote,

> Whom should I turn to
> If not the one whose darkness
> Is darker than night, the only one
> Who keeps vigil with no candle
> And is not afraid—
> The deep one, whose being I trust,
> For it breaks through the earth into trees,
> And rises,
> When I bow my head,
> Faint as a fragrance from the soil.

5.

The Ripples of Good-Bye

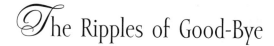

A mighty flame
followeth a tiny spark.

Dante

Major loss is never just one event. Like a stone thrown into a pond, the ripples extend . . . and extend . . . and extend. In my book *Nobody's Child Anymore*, I point out that after adult children lose the second parent, the family home is often sold, so the family's gathering center is lost. When a child dies, statistics show that grief brings down many marriages. When you lose a job, financial fears can further stress a troubled marriage. When you make a geographical move, your kids may act out their distress.

In the national tragedy of September 11, 2001, the initial loss of lives was only the beginning. There were vast psychological and economic aftershocks, some occurring in ways no one could have foretold.

I began learning about loss's ripple effect after John died.

Losing Your Role

"Hi, is your mom there?"

I had called a Navy friend, and her daughter answered the phone.

"No, she and dad went to a squadron party."

A party? For the squadron? And I wasn't invited?

I felt as if I were shrinking. Holding the phone but growing smaller and smaller like the little girl I'd once been, standing alone on the playground because I was new and didn't have friends, didn't belong, and was all alone.

They held a squadron party and didn't invite me.

John was dead. I wasn't a squadron wife anymore.

I don't belong.

But if I don't belong in the Navy . . . where do I belong?

Still holding the phone, with only a dial tone now, I slid to the floor and huddled against the wall. My daughter Allison came in a few minutes later. She saw me on the floor.

"Are you okay, Mom? You look funny."

I'm a mom. I'm supposed to be in charge. But I don't feel like a mom. I feel like—and quickly, before my daughter could see, I pushed up from the floor and ran to my bedroom, slamming the door and throwing myself across the bed. I didn't so much cry as sob. Hard, hurting sobs that rose up from someplace so deep I hadn't even known it was there.

I'm alone. I don't belong. And I'm scared to be alone. Please, John, don't be dead. Come back. Come back.

a helping hand

It was later, much much later, when I learned that my feelings that night were normal. Everyone who experiences a major lifestyle shift will feel a loss of role or place. Your familiar context and the way you define yourself are both gone.

Divorce or death takes away your couple status, so you're left out of couples' socializing. If you retire or lose your job, you may find that your fellow workers, the people you thought of as friends, were merely work-neighbors. Once you're out of the neighborhood, you're no longer part of their lives.

If you find your self-image in your title—*Mother, Principal, President, Daughter, Manager*—you may not know how to define yourself when the title is gone.

No wonder you feel disoriented.

In *Necessary Losses*, Judith Viorst wrote, "Each transition leads to termination of a previous life structure and each termination is an ending, a process of separation or loss."

The transition period is difficult. For centuries, spiritual writers have referred to it as "the desert experience." The desert, metaphorically, is the empty, seemingly barren, in-between time—the transition between what was and what will be.

Of course you feel uncomfortable! You're no longer who you were, and you haven't yet learned who you will be. In his book *Transitions*, William Bridges calls it "a kind of limbo when a person floats free between two worlds."

Part of establishing a new identity is to recognize what part of your old identity existed primarily in your head. It's also the time to look carefully at your image and ask, "How much was authentically me?" How much was the image you created to live up to others' expectations? If you're willing to tolerate a period of discomfort, you may find a freedom to become more truly who you were meant to be.

Realize that it will take time. Don't plunge into action—any action—just to be doing something. Especially don't plunge into a relationship. Studies have found it takes about two years before someone widowed or divorced is truly ready for remarriage.

This is a good time to try out different images. Write lists to assess your achievements, your skills, and what you enjoy most. Take a class in something you've always wanted to learn. Try a new sport such as bicycling or skiing. And be patient.

Trappist monk Thomas Merton wrote a powerful prayer of faith that speaks to transitions. It begins: "My God, I have no idea where I am going. I do not see the road ahead of me. I cannot know for certain where it will end . . . [but] I know you will lead me by the right road though I may know nothing about it. Therefore, I will trust you always."

Can these words comfort and encourage you?

Innocent Victims

One of the many decisions I made after John died was to return to school. Now that I was the family breadwinner, I knew I needed skills.

With financial aid, I finished the education I'd interrupted when John and I married, and in 1972, with my newly minted graduate degree, I accepted a career position in Kansas City. It felt like a major step forward in rebuilding my life and my children's lives.

What I didn't realize was how disruptive it would be for my kids to move from San Diego to a strange city in the Midwest. Our move meant they lost their familiar neighborhood where their friends had known their dad. They lost their extended family of my parents and brothers. They were flung into a new environment with a single working mom and all the stresses of that change.

Allison, shy and already nervous about starting seventh grade, went for what we thought was a routine physical. Instead, the doctor diagnosed scoliosis and prescribed a gawky, uncomfortable neck-to-hip brace. Allison burst into tears. "I'll look like a dork and never make friends!"

Fifth-grader John kicked out angrily at a world that had robbed him of his father, and then forced him to move to a stupid place with cornfields where kids sneered, "My father says Vietnam is a bad war and your father deserved to die."

Third-grader Andy had earlier been diagnosed with learning disabilities and hyperactivity. (Today, we'd call it ADHD.) He, too, felt "different." When a teacher asked why he never smiled, Andy replied solemnly, "I tried on a smile, but when I looked in the mirror, it didn't fit."

a helping hand

In the wake of a loss, you may have no other choice. You know your decision will create difficult ripples in your child's life, but still, you have to do it. A job transfer. A divorce. A home sold in the wake of an economic downturn.

Try to stay attuned to your child's real feelings, and make it clear that it's okay to express sadness, sorrow, anger, or fear.

Sometimes adults find it hard to tolerate a child's pain, especially if they know their decisions are the cause of it, so they will give an unspoken message:

"Don't show me your grief." But when children's feelings are ignored or misunderstood, those feelings, like chemicals in ground water, rise later to affect their adult relationships and choices.

A Child's Sorrow

Though she was only five, Mary knew that something was very wrong. Her baby brother, whose crib used to be in her room, was sick, and her mommy didn't have time anymore to hug Mary or read to her. She didn't even seem to *see* Mary. And when Mary went looking for her big sister, her sister yelled at her to go away.

Mary sat in the living room all by herself, listening to the loud ticks of the grandfather clock and the noise of cicadas outside the open windows. She knew about cicadas because her father was a naturalist who often went on expeditions to far-off places. He was on an expedition now and people were trying to reach him. Mary leaned on the table where a framed photo of her father sat. She put her face up close to his and wished her father would come home.

All at once, a door slammed. Footsteps clattered on the stairs and she heard her big sister's voice. "Mary, where are you?" Before Mary could answer, her sister appeared in the doorway. She looked angry. "Our brother just died. Go to your room." When Mary didn't move, her sister screamed, "Do you hear me? Go to your room!"

Years and years later, as Mary recalled that evening to me, her voice shook with remembered pain. "I climbed into my bed, and waited and waited, but no one came . . . and finally, I fell asleep, still waiting for someone to come in and hug me."

As an adult, Mary understands—intellectually— that her childhood home was awash in grief that night. Her two-year-old brother had just died of brain cancer. Her mother's pain was so deep, she couldn't find extra space for her little girl just then. Her big sister, who wasn't really so big—only ten years old—didn't know what to do other than to order her little sister to bed. The adult side of Mary understands. Deep inside, though, a little-girl part of her felt bereft and abandoned for many years.

a helping hand

Mary's story is another example of how easily children's needs get lost when families are overwhelmed by grief. Give your children information in words appropriate to their ages. Don't fall to pieces in front of them, but don't try to hide your own sadness. Children's radar for feelings is extraordinarily sensitive. Let them know that it's okay to be sad. Most of all, reassure them that they are not abandoned, and that, despite the loss occurring in your family, you will be there for them.

You may also need to ask yourself, especially if your grief seems more intense than you expected: *Does my grief today have roots in a past loss?* "Grief knows no time," said psychiatrist Louis Forman. If grief work is not completed, it leaves threads dangling in the fabric of your life, and they will be pulled again by a later loss. Life calls on us to face our losses, say good-bye, mourn, and complete them.

Memory

Maggie saw grief swamp two of her closest friends. One was a divorce flameout whose bitterness had etched such unhappy lines in her face, it was hard to be around her. Another friend, who suffered a double loss when her husband filed for divorce after their only child died of leukemia, became almost catatonic.

So when her own six-foot-five, "healthy-as-a-horse" husband died a shockingly sudden death at age fifty-six, Maggie knew one thing. She wouldn't let grief swallow her. Absolutely not! "I researched what to do as a widow," Maggie told me. She's a journalist and knows how to research. "I did everything people told me. Joined support groups. Went to exercise class. Lost weight. Got counseling. Invested wisely. Stayed in touch with old friends. Made new friends. Took a trip to Africa. Repainted my bedroom. And you know what?"

"What?"

Her eyes filled. Resolutely she smiled, blinked, refusing to let tears fall. But her smile held an ironic twist. "Everyone complimented me on how well I was doing, and assured me I'd soon start feeling better, because look how busy I was, doing all the right things. And for awhile, it seemed like people were right. Then, nearly two years after Bob died, I saw a bunch of guys playing pick-up basketball, and one looked like Bob from the back, and suddenly it hit me. 'Wait. This is forever! He's gone forever. And even if I do all the right things, I still can't bring him back!'" Her voice dropped. "It made me so angry! No matter what I do, I can never bring him back!'"

a helping hand

In her determination to do all the "right things" as a widow, Maggie forgot one important detail: loss hurts. Whatever you have lost—a job, a beloved person, a marriage, a particular environment—you may do everything "right" to take charge of your recovery in a healthy way, and pain can still assault you when you least expect it.

Poet Edna St. Vincent Millay expressed this poignantly:

> There are a hundred places where I fear
> To go—so with his memory they brim
> And entering with relief some quiet place
> Where never fell his foot or shone his face
> I say "There is no memory of him here!"
> And so stand stricken, so remembering him.

So, now and again, when you least expect it, you, too, will stand stricken as Maggie did outside the basketball court. Then it's a little like falling. Experts say that if you stiffen and fight a fall, you are more likely to get hurt physically than if you relax your body and let the fall happen. So, let the pain happen. Feel it, don't fight it. Have faith that it will pass. Believe that you will pick yourself up again. And you will.

Nostalgia

I remember my surprise as I browsed one of the super-sized bookstores eight years after my divorce. At the magazine rack, I picked up a ski magazine. As I paged through it, I saw pictures of the Colorado mountains where my ex-spouse and I had lived and skied in the last four years of our marriage. Unexpectedly, I was gripped by a nostalgic yearning. *Wait a minute!* I thought. *I like my life today. Why this sudden sadness?* As I put the magazine back on the shelf, I realized: even though my marriage had been foundering, the mountains themselves had offered an exhilarating environment in which to live. I recalled the rush of pleasure as I stood at the top of a ski slope, looking out across snow-capped peaks. I remembered the creak of a chair lift in the crystalline silence. I remembered how special it felt to know I was not a tourist, but a "local," someone who actually lived in the mountains.

a helping hand

Moving on from loss is never a straight line. An emotional tug can recur without warning long after you thought you had put the past behind you. Like Maggie, you may see someone who reminds you of your beloved. Or, like me, you may feel sudden nostalgia for a certain place. Or a lifestyle. A former fighter pilot who left the Navy to run a successful family business told me that even though he is quite happy with his life in Oklahoma, he feels nostalgic every time he sees The Blue Angels, the Navy's precision flying team, perform. "It's like a fist in the gut. A reminder that once upon a time, I knew how to fly planes like that."

But be careful about nostalgia, especially for relationships or situations that were not harmonious. Memory may edit your experience until you forget the unpleasant part and "remember" good stuff that wasn't even there. Such editing is fine if it keeps you from clinging to bitter resentment. Just be sure to acknowledge what is good in your life today, and don't yearn for what, in fact, never really existed.

Ceremony

Rituals help establish the reality of loss. John's body was lost at sea, but we still held a memorial service. To make his presence felt, I went through the letters he had written me, and out of his own words, composed a eulogy that expressed how he felt about his children, his family, his friends, and his commitment to serving his country.

My father, a retired Air Force colonel, stood ramrod straight in the Navy chapel, and in a measured voice, read John's words. There were muffled sobs as friends and comrades listened. *You are here with us*, I thought. *Through your words, we feel you, John.*
Then, as we walked outside, four fighter jets appeared in formation on the horizon. They hurtled across the blue cloudless sky until one jet spun away from the others and flew, ever higher and alone, toward the heavens. "Good-bye," I whispered.

When Laurie and Don buried their infant twin sons who died within weeks of their premature birth, they placed in Robert's casket his first baby gift, a teddy bear. When his brother Thomas' coffin was lowered into the tiny grave, Laurie gently dropped on it one white rose for Thomas and another white rose for Robert. The ceremony helped Laurie and Don say to their sons and to themselves, "Your lives were brief, but they counted, and you are loved."

A friend, whose very elderly, atheist mother had requested no funeral, held a memorial service anyway in her own church. "I needed to say good-bye," she said. "And even if Mom didn't care, I needed to acknowledge my mother's life to my friends and family."

a helping hand

Reality must be acknowledged before mourning can begin. It's important to mark the passage of what or who you leave behind. As grief expert Helen Fitzgerald wrote, funerals allow you to say, "I care about you" or, "I love you" or even, "I'm sorry." Without good-bye, there is a lack of closure.

Other losses are also helped with a farewell rite. My friend Dottie invited several close friends to her lakeside home for a post-divorce ceremony. They read aloud poems and prayers selected by Dottie. They listened to music. At the end, in somber finality, they watched as Dottie threw her wedding ring into the lake.

Another friend held a private ritual after losing her job. She tossed papers from her old job into her fireplace and watched them burn. Then she lit a circle of candles around her resume to signal the energy and light that would result in a new, even better job. A church service may also help you find necessary closure.

To acknowledge an ending can help you eventually find a new beginning. And to believe that one day, though it may seem impossible at this moment, you will rediscover life's joy.

6.

Seeking Support

The world breaks everyone and afterward
many are strong at the broken places.

Ernest Hemingway

*V*ery few people can recover alone from significant loss. We feel an instinctive need to seek comfort and support from our fellow human beings. Think about major public griefs. Princess Diana's untimely death. The Columbine school massacre. The September 11 terrorist attacks.

In the wake of those events, strangers became non-strangers. People leaned on each other's shoulders, commiserated with one another, placed flowers and notes in spontaneous shrines. E-mails flowed. Telephone lines lit up. Houses of worship filled.

Endlessly, we asked one another, "Where were you when . . . ?" "Can you believe it happened?" We clung to our televisions, watching images over and over again, feeling somehow connected with others around the globe who were similarly watching.

And it isn't only tragic death that prompts us to reach out. Increasingly, people with debilitating diseases—cancer, ALS, diabetes—find comfort and inspiration in support groups.

A California career coach said, after working with fifteen hundred people who had lost jobs, "The magic of recovery begins when people are ready to reach out to others."

At a 1998 scientific convention, a researcher reported: "People who lack good personal networks are more at risk, health-wise, than people who smoke."

When you suffer a loss, support is crucial.

Support comes from *people*. Support also comes from your *mind*, and the way you choose to think. It comes from special *places* that speak to your soul. It comes from healing *activities* that buoy you. And support comes powerfully from *prayer*. In this chapter, we'll look at the support we receive from people and prayer. In the following chapters we'll examine the other sources of support.

Christmas Tree

In December, three months after my husband John died, my uncle shipped me a Christmas tree: a tall, beautiful blue spruce. It smelled as if freshly cut, and all of us—the three children and I—breathed deeply its aroma of pine-scented, high mountain forests. "It smells like the camping trips we went on with Daddy," said Allison.

"It does, doesn't it?"

The spruce tree was tall, and it took some maneuvering to get it from our porch into the living room. "I'll get the tree stand," shouted my son John. He remembered where it was in our garage, and brought out a green-and-red metal contraption. I tried to poke the tree's trunk into the stand. It didn't fit. Then I saw pins that could be let out to widen the tree stand. I pulled them out and tried again.

"Mommy! Watch out!"

The tree was toppling, falling onto the sofa. Its branches brushed a crystal bowl off the coffee table.

I sighed in consternation. John had always set up our trees and wrapped them in lights. Then, and only then, was it my turn to pull out the box of ornaments: the special ones we had bought in Germany; the red and blue and gold glass balls from Wal-Mart; and the paper-and-paste ones made by the kids.

John had set up the tree, but now he was gone.

Now I was responsible.

I wiped my brow. "Boys, you hold the tree up. Allison, help me poke it in the stand." They tried. I tried. Again, the heavy tree toppled over.

Thirty minutes later, pine needles nestled on the floor, between sofa cushions, on tables, and still I had not succeeded in getting the tree into the stand.

My eyes filled. The angry tears came so quickly, so unexpectedly, I didn't have time to hide them from the children. I just began crying. Allison's lip trembled. "Mommy, don't cry."

"I'm sorry, honey. I—I'll go see if Mr. McVay can help us."

I ran into the night. It was dark by now. I looked up and shook my fist at the stars.

"You should be here, John! I need you! I'm supposed to do it all, and I can't even put up the damn Christmas tree! How will we manage without you? How?" The tree seemed a symbol of all John had provided in our lives: the sense of being cared for, the laughter, the loving arm around my shoulders, the sharing, the capabilities he had that I didn't.

"I can't do it," I whimpered.

I rang my neighbor's doorbell.

He came to the door, a balding, slightly over-weight math teacher.

I started sobbing. Hiccupy sobs and disjointed words, so he had to say, again and again, "I'm sorry, you say you can't do . . . what? The tree? Your life? I'm sorry . . . what?"

In the end, he seemed to understand, and he came out of his house and walked across the side-walk into our living room. The children were hud-dled around the fallen tree. Mr. McVay, ever the teacher, said in hearty tones, "All right now, kids. Look lively. We've got a tree to put up!" As if a but-ton had been pushed, the children came to life. In less than five minutes, Mr. McVay affixed the tree firmly in its stand. I stared, transfixed. How had he done it?

We moved chairs so he could maneuver the tree to a spot in front of the living room window. "There, now it's all ready for decorating."

"Thank you," my words stumbled, "I really lost it—"

He patted my shoulder. "I know," he said, and somehow we both knew he wasn't talking about just this night or this event.

"Call on me again. Anytime," he said.

I closed the front door and breathed in the aroma of the tree. In the distance, as if carried across a mountain meadow, I seemed to hear John's laugh.

"Well," I said. "It's a little late tonight, but tomor-row, kids, we'll decorate our tree."

a helping hand

So many times I've heard people say, after a loss, "The person who helped me most was someone I never expected." You, too, may find this to be so. A neighbor or someone you knew casually at work begins showing up on a regular basis. Maybe someone who's had a similar experience becomes a helpful new friend.

The reverse is also true. A person you expected to be there for you may be unable to handle your grief. Almost everyone who experiences death, divorce, or job loss reports that some people drop out of their lives. It's not personal. It comes from another's fear or insecurity. One friend excused herself from seeing me by saying, "I'm sorry, Barbara. I don't do death."

Accept help from those who want to help. Be open to the unexpected person who reaches out to you. Try and forgive those who drop away. Realize that it's not you they're rejecting, but your circumstances.

"Please Help"

In San Diego, my friend Marna was only fifty when her cancer metastasized. As a former military wife, she had friends around the world, and immediately, she wrote to them. "I need you," she wrote. "I need you to pray for me and call me and send me letters and let me know you love me."

Her friends responded and Marna lived, joyously and nearly pain-free, a year longer than her doctors thought she would. I was sad when she died, yet I'm convinced the support she asked for and received helped extend her life and made her ultimate letting go far more peaceful.

Another man, whom I'll call Joe, e-mailed friends and asked them to join his "buffalo herd." With ironic humor, he said, "Buffaloes were considered nearly extinct, but now, they're back. My doctors are telling me I'm nearly extinct. I refuse to believe it. If you join my herd you'll have to promise to send me good wishes, good humor, and lots of inspiration. No negatives allowed!"

Joe lived six years longer than his doctors had predicted, and his concept of a supportive buffalo herd was picked up and used by cancer patients in many parts of the country.

a helping hand

Do you need a buffalo herd? The American psyche is fiercely independent, which makes it hard for some to admit their need. You may feel weak, embarrassed, or afraid of imposing. Maybe you're ashamed, or afraid to ask because you might be rejected.

Yet so many times people yearn to help and don't know what to do. By letting someone know *how* to help you, you do the person a kindness. Don't be afraid to ask for help.

Been There

In the dark winter of 1968, I sat in my living room, a glass of wine beside me. Shadows played on the walls, cast by the reflection of a street lamp. It was nearly 2 a.m. and I was listening to an audio tape of my dead husband singing. John was well-loved for his songs and stories, and on various occasions friends had taped him. Now, as I heard his rich, strong voice, I felt as if my body might explode with pain. I felt desperate for something—anything—to help me.

Abruptly, I grabbed the telephone and punched in a phone number.

Millie's sleepy voice said, "Hello?"

Two years before, Millie's Navy pilot husband had died in a fiery plane crash over the Mojave Desert. We lived only a few blocks apart in San Diego, but were more social acquaintances than close friends.

But Millie was a widow. She knew what I was going through, and my need was so great, I didn't care that I was calling her at two o'clock in the morning.

"I'll be right over," she said.

Fifteen minutes later, she walked into my living room. Gently, she turned off the tape recorder. "It's too soon, Barb. You can't play those tapes yet. Give yourself more time."

We talked until four. Millie told me things about her own mourning that I had never heard her say before. She gave me practical advice. And mostly, she gave me hope: "It does get better, Barb."

Others had said that, but Millie *knew*. I trusted what she said.

That night began a friendship that has lasted to this day. Mutual need brought us together. Both of us had three children to raise. Both of us went back to school. Together, we began to take our kids camping. By ourselves, we went on a ski trip, giggling like two teenagers. Mostly, we talked. My need to talk helped Millie, who was more reticent than I to express her own feelings. In the end, we helped each other mourn.

a helping hand

Look around. Whatever your experience, there are others who have gone through something similar. Someone else who has experienced divorce, or a job loss, or who knows what it's like to lose physical mobility . . . those are the people who can help you— and whom you can help—in ways no one else can.

In recent years, there's been an explosion of support groups—from Twelve-Step programs, to Survivors After Suicide, to Parents of Murdered Children, to Tough Love, to Professionals in Transition, to Alzheimer's Caregivers, to groups that support an incredible number of diseases.

If you can't find a support group that meets your needs, consider starting one. With e-mail and web sites, it's even easier today, and not confined to one geographical area.

Help From the Internet

After her divorce, Susan, a Minnesota nurse, felt as if her life were at a crossroads, both psychologically and spiritually. She no longer felt in tune with the Lutheran church of her childhood or the Methodist church she had attended with her ex-spouse, yet she was hungry for something.

"I wanted a relationship with God," she said, "but not necessarily within the confines of a church." She sought the assistance of a spiritual director on the Internet who nurtures clients on "the path their souls choose."

The Internet also helped Ginny. Three months after her baby died, she put this message on a grief site's bulletin board: "I want my baby! Sometimes it seems like I held him just moments ago, like I can still feel his breath on my neck. Other days it seems like I've been mourning him forever.

"I can't talk to my husband right now. I tried, but he's on a different path, and we're not connecting. Today in the shower, I picked up the washcloth I used in my baby's bath, and I held it to my face and cried and cried. My sweet baby is gone and all I have are memories. It's so unfair!"

Ginny's heartbroken message brought loving responses from other mothers who grieved for their lost babies.

a helping hand

When I went to the Internet search engine *Google.com* and tapped in the words "bereavement and grief," Google found 57,000 possible links. Support for every imaginable need is available with a click of your mouse. *Griefnet.org* is one of the best for someone who is mourning a death. There are others for job loss and divorce.

You may find it easier to express yourself in the anonymity of a web site chat room or message board. Some people do. Or you may use the web as an adjunct to your real-time friends. Such support didn't exist five years ago. It offers a real benefit, is available 24/7, and is worth exploring.

Small Kindnesses

Sometimes the most meaningful help is not something large but something that, on the surface, seems very small. One day, John's friend Stan, another Navy pilot, showed up at my front door carrying a grocery sack full of light bulbs. He smiled and pointed to my darkened porch light. "I bring you light!"

he proclaimed. After replacing my porch light, he replaced several other burned-out bulbs in the house. But he brought far more than the wattage of light bulbs. I found myself laughing for the first time in weeks when Stan hoisted five-year-old Andrew onto his shoulders and trotted him around the living room shouting "Giddyap!"

Later, I thought how compassionate it was of Stan to notice that my house had grown as shadowed as my life. He couldn't return my husband to me, but he could brighten my home—and in that small act, he could testify that he cared.

A friend who had to sell her home in the wake of a divorce described how her neighbor had appeared as the moving van was driving away. "I'll go through each room with you and hold your hand as you say good-bye," said the neighbor. No one could prevent the loss of her home. But by holding my friend's hand, her neighbor reminded her that she still had what mattered most: people in her life who cared.

a helping hand

It's possible to feel so overwhelmed with grief that you don't notice when small acts of compassion are extended. Open your heart to see the little ways in which someone has reached out. Small kindnesses cannot staunch your loss, but can help you feel less alone. Poet Emily Dickinson understood this when she wrote

> By Chivalries as tiny
> A Blossom, or a Book
> The seeds of smiles are planted—
> Which Blossom in the dark.

Intercessory Prayer

Army Lieutenant Colonel Brian Birdwell was meeting with two coworkers in his Pentagon office on September 11, 2001. He excused himself to go to the restroom. Before he could return, one of the jets hijacked by terrorists slammed into the Pentagon. Birdwell's office was a direct hit, and both his coworkers were killed.

When Birdwell stumbled into the hallway, he was engulfed in flames. He cried out to God, then fell. Miraculously, he fell directly beneath a sprinkler. Even so, his arms, hands, and ears were so badly burned that when he tried to get up he could only cry out again. Rescuers heard, and within minutes, carried him from the building. Someone commandeered a vehicle and rushed him to a nearby hospital.

Col. Birdwell's wife Mel was at home that morning, home-schooling their son Matt. The phone rang. A friend from their church cried, "Turn on the TV! Something terrible has happened."

As soon as she saw the televised images, Mel knelt with her son and prayed. "I felt God's peace as I prayed," she said. "Even if Brian didn't survive, I knew he was with God."

At the hospital, Brian's head was swollen "to the size of a boulder." The fire had burned clear through the muscles on his arms and hands. In the next ten weeks, he would endure twenty surgeries and skin grafts.

"Brian's not a man to cry, but the pain was so intense in the whirlpool baths that tears streamed down his face and he cried, 'I can't do this!' It ripped my heart out to hear him," said Mel.

But Brian Birdwell survived his ordeal. His doctors and nurses helped, but just as important, Mel believes, were the prayers of the four thousand members of their church family.

a helping hand

Mel Birdwell showed an instant reliance on God when she dropped to her knees in prayer. She trusted in God's mercy "even if Brian didn't survive," and her faith was strengthened by the prayers of her church community.

Surveys show that eighty percent of Americans believe that prayer's power can improve the course of illness, and solid evidence is appearing to back this belief. In 2000, The National Institutes of Health launched a five-year study to determine if prayer intervention can improve the health of cancer patients.

Larry Dossey, M.D., in his book *Healing Words: The Power of Prayer and the Practice of Medicine* reports on various studies related to prayer and healing. One reviewer said this about Dr. Dossey's book: "The science is so solid [about prayer's value] that it is criminally negligent for physicians not to recommend it. There is no cost except for time, so it makes no logical sense why someone would not utilize this resource."

Is prayer a resource you should try? God has no timetable, so it doesn't matter if you haven't prayed before. Your prayers count now.

Serendipity

Prayer helped me in the wake of losing my job. In the 1980s, no one talked about *downsizing*, but advertising was known as a notoriously fickle field. I'd worked as an ad agency copywriter for three years when Josh, the creative director, beckoned me into his office one Friday.

I thought he wanted to discuss a campaign for a new client, but he fiddled with a paperweight, touched the collar of his blue denim shirt, and then said, "Barb, I'm letting you go."

For a moment, I simply didn't understand. Then it hit. He was firing me!

"I'm sorry," said Josh. "I'm sure you'll find another spot."

When I pressed him for details, he was vague. He agreed my work was good but spoke about "changing agency needs . . . not the right fit . . . ," all the while leading me to the door. I slunk down the hall, feeling as if I wore a scarlet letter. A for Awful.

Inside my office, with the door closed, I squeezed my hands into angry fists. In sudden rage, I swept papers and my purse off my desk. As they scattered to the floor, a small scrap fluttered from my purse. I picked it up. It was the phone number of a Catholic retreat center. I had copied it down several weeks earlier. How peculiar to find it now. I pushed it back into my purse, and burst into tears.

The next morning, when I came across the paper again, it seemed like such an odd coincidence that I reached for the phone. I was connected to a small retreat house in the heart of the city. Yes, they were holding a weekend retreat, and it just so happened that a sudden cancellation had left one spot open.

I found someone to stay with my kids, and went.

If you asked me today to locate the retreat house, I'm not sure I could. I don't remember the name of the nun who ran it. But I do remember the way her calm, measured voice smoothed my angry, choked tears. She directed me to the words in Psalm 10: "You hear, O Lord, the desire of the afflicted . . . in the Lord

I take refuge." She encouraged me to stay open to all possibilities, and assured me that my talents would find a new home.

When I left on Sunday morning, she clasped my hand. "Every ending is also a beginning," she murmured. "You'll find a blessing in this event." I squeezed her hand, and as I drove home, I could almost believe her.

a helping hand

Serendipity is defined as "making a desirable discovery by accident." The definition for grace is "the freely given favor and love of God." Surely the two are connected. Don't dismiss divine gift as mere coincidence. The Archbishop of Canterbury once said, "The more I pray, the fewer coincidences there are in my life."

Stay open to noticing—and appreciating—God's favors.

Perhaps you pick up a book and it falls open to a page that is especially helpful. Or when you're feeling lonely, a friend you haven't talked to in months calls. Or you think you've turned the wrong way, and instead it takes you to a new opportunity. God's grace often shows up in such wonderful serendipity moments. Pay attention. And respond.

A Surprising Result

For Valerie, support made a crucial difference in how she recovered from a loss no eighteen-year-old would ever expect. On October 16, a sunlit day in eastern Washington, Valerie was perched behind her friend Harvey on his motorcycle. The two college freshmen were headed to Kenniwick, their hometown, for a weekend visit.

As they neared the outskirts of town, a car crested the hill on the two-lane highway. Behind the wheel was a sixteen-year-old boy who had gotten his driver's license just a few weeks earlier. Whether from inexperience or inattention, he hurtled straight toward their motorcycle. Valerie screamed. There was a blistering sound of metal on metal, an explosive screech, and the bike went down. Harvey and Valerie tumbled downhill into a plowed field.

A passing truck driver saw what happened, jumped out of his truck, tore down the hill, and put on makeshift tourniquets. Valerie, still conscious but in shock, mumbled, "I lost my leg, didn't I?" The truck driver slowly nodded. Sirens shrieked. An ambulance arrived and paramedics took over.

Valerie's leg had been severed above the knee.

More than her pain, what she remembers most about the aftermath were the well-wishers who jammed the hospital. It seemed as if everyone in the small town of Kenniwick responded to the plight of the two local teenagers. Valerie's parents stayed at her bedside and friends flocked home from various colleges to visit and cheer her.

After her release from the hospital, a newspaper story went out over the wires, and mail poured in from the rest of the country.

"We're thinking of you," wrote some.

"You can make it through this," wrote others.

And still others wrote: "Hearing about you has helped me put my own problems in perspective."

It wasn't easy. Valerie experienced phantom limb pain. She spent anxious moments learning to walk with a prosthesis. She had a tiring regimen of daily exercises. And there was her own shuddering comment the first time she took a bath: "Oh, it's so ugly! I can't stand to look at it!"

Her mother, who had helped her into the bath, responded very matter-of-factly. "Valerie, it's your leg. It's not ugly. It is what it is. You'll get used to it."

It is what it is.

Before her accident, Valerie was known as a "worrier." Although academically gifted, she often felt anxious. Then the motorcycle accident occurred.

"Oddly enough," Valerie told me, many years later, "my accident was so terrible that once I came through *that*, I felt as if I could handle *anything*. My anxiety was gone. I emerged stronger as a result of losing my leg."

a helping hand

The way neighbors and strangers rallied around helped Valerie. But what made a crucial difference was her mother's practical, no-nonsense attitude. *"It's your leg. It is what it is. You'll get used to it."* Her words allowed no debilitating self-pity. They reminded Valerie that she was more than her severed limb. It was up to her to adapt.

If you have experienced a physical change, through illness, age, paralysis, or some other loss, find support from people like Valerie's mom. Don't let anyone try to make you overly dependent or encourage you to feel sorry for yourself.

The more you accept yourself, the stronger you'll feel, and the more accepting other people will be. You're more than what you lost. Look for others who agree.

7.

$\mathscr{S}$upportive Thoughts

As a one thinks in his heart, so he is.

Proverbs

The last of the human freedoms is to choose one's attitude in a given set of circumstances, to choose one's own way.

Viktor Frankl

he experience of loss forces us out of life as we have known it. Coping often demands a new way of thinking, a shift of attitude and perception.

When psychiatrist Jerry Jampolsky began working with children who had life-threatening illnesses, he developed what he called *attitudinal healing*, a way of changing the way you look at the world. Even if

99

the body doesn't heal, healing the mind enables a person to live with a greater sense of peace despite the outer circumstances.

This is not a new idea. Healing of thoughts is part of all religions. Eastern wisdom says, "Cease to do evil, learn to do good, and cleanse your own heart." Western thought says, "As a man thinketh in his heart, so is he," and, "Seek ye first God's kingdom and righteousness." Quantum physicist Ford Allen Wolf put it in scientific terms when he said the universe doesn't exist independent of the thought of the observer. How you think will shape what you notice and how you respond.

Write, Write, Write

One of the best ways to get in touch with what you're thinking and feeling is to keep a journal. I call my small, hardcover books "Letters to God."

My first "letter to God" was written in the wake of a heated argument when my husband John was still alive. It was one of those quarrels that lingers in the air. Afterward, we walked gingerly around one another, barely speaking. I yearned for our impasse to end but stubbornly thought he should make the first move. Then I noticed on my night table the small, blank-page book a friend had given me as a gift two months earlier.

I picked up the book and a pen and tentatively wrote, *"Dear God . . . "* and then, surprised at how quickly the words flowed, *"I'm feeling so sad. I want John to end our quarrel and tell me he loves me, but again this morning, he left without a smile or a kiss."* My handwriting grew more agitated until, three pages later, I slowly concluded, *"Maybe I should stop feeling so self-righteous. Aren't we told to turn the other cheek? Help me, oh God, to take the first step."*

When John came home that evening, the weight of our silence felt as suffocating as the air before a thunderstorm. But my "letter to God" had stayed with me, and although it was hard to force the words out, I said, "John, I'm sorry for my part in our argument." John's face, so impassive just a moment before, abruptly changed. He reached for me. "I'm sorry too," he said. It had simply taken one of us to make the first move.

Through writing, it seemed as if God entered my consciousness, not to give answers but to show me something I already had inside.

When I lost my job, my written words seethed. *"Dear God, I'm angry! You failed me! I worked hard! This isn't fair!"* After several pages of angry diatribe, though, my tone softened. Eventually I wrote, *"OK God, I know I'm not the only one who has lost a job. But I can't afford to be out of work and I'm scared. Please. Help!"*

It was a relief to realize I could rage at God. Once I acknowledged my anger, I was able to find the hurt and fear that hid behind it. Becoming God's pen pal has helped me review, process, and discover a more positive way to handle life's struggles and losses. Whenever I reread my journals, I see what a guiding hand God has had in my life, even when I didn't notice it was there.

a helping hand

When you put feelings into words, you're better able to understand and deal with them.

In a 1999 report on journal writing, the Journal of the American Medical Association said patients who wrote about their stressful experiences "had clinically relevant changes in health status . . . beyond those attributable to standard medical care." A job out-placement counselor in Seattle noticed that clients who kept journals found faster closure after losing their jobs, and—interestingly enough—found new jobs sooner than those who didn't journal.

You don't have to write every day, but make a commitment to spend a few minutes, at least two or three times a week. Start each journal entry with the words "Dear God." Or, if you prefer, "To the Universal Creator." Or, "To my Higher Self." Be *honest* in what you write, whether you're mad, sad, or glad.

Reread your entries a few months later, and you'll see how far you have come in processing your grief.

Crayon Comfort

Years after I started journaling, I discovered it also helps to *draw pictures* of your emotions.

One day while shopping, shortly after I separated from my second husband Bill, I bought a box of crayons for my grandson. When I got home, I found a biting letter from Bill on my fax machine. My stomach churned, and I was ready to write an angry reply when I spied the crayons. Instead of writing, I began to draw.

I'd read about such drawings in Dr. Bernie Siegel's book *Love, Medicine and Miracles.* He asked cancer patients to draw pictures that showed how they felt about their lives. Their pictures offered insight into patients' attitudes, which in turn impacted their healing.

I dumped out the box of crayons so they spilled across the table. So many colors. Purple. Blue. Yellow. Red. I'm left-handed, but deliberately I began to draw with my right, or non-dominant, hand.

I made slashing lines with the purple crayon. Up. Down. Right. Left. It looked like a box. Inside the box, I drew a red balloon—then, from some place other than my conscious mind, the balloon became a face with a rounded O—a mouth open in a silent scream. Blue dots cascaded down the face. Now the face became a head, attached to a rough stick figure. It was crouched inside the box. Outside, another bigger figure leered with an angry expression.

With my left hand, the one I ordinarily use, I wrote, "This picture shows. . . . " My words flowed. I had drawn my little-girl self, the child part of me that I called Barbara Helen (because my grandmother called me that). Barbara Helen was hunched over, trapped inside a box. She was scared and sad. Tears (the blue dots) poured down her cheeks. Outside the box the giant figure of her ex-husband yelled at her. She felt boxed in and afraid. She didn't know how to get out of her box.

It wasn't a very happy picture, but it gave me insight into how boxed in I felt at that moment. Soon I was drawing several times a week. My crude, rough pictures spoke in visual symbols, just as dreams do. Each time that I wrote what "this picture shows" I gained new understanding about hidden parts of myself.

Eventually, as I continued to process my feelings, my drawings became happier. I began drawing butterflies and trees that were heavy with fruit, streams of blue water and paths that curved upward. Barbara Helen began to smile.

a helping hand

You, too, can practice this simple art therapy, and the results may astonish you. In losses that carry feelings of anger, betrayal, shame, or guilt, such as a divorce or job loss, drawing from the right side of the brain helps tap into your unconscious, and identifies feelings that may not have consciously surfaced.

All it takes is a piece of paper, a box of crayons, and a willingness to relax and draw whatever seems to come. Try to suspend your conscious mind—that's why it helps to draw with your non-dominant hand. See what emerges. Don't force it. Then write what your drawing says to you. You may be surprised at what you learn. And you'll feel better.

In Topeka, Kansas, Elizabeth Layton was sixty-eight when she began to draw with colored pencils. Her drawings pulled her out of a thirty-year depression and eventually attracted the favorable notice of art critics. You may not become the darling of art critics, but your drawings can show you some important things about yourself.

The Words of Others

When I stayed with my mom during her final months of life, I haunted the library near her home. I've always been an avid reader, maybe because I grew up before TV. I look to books for comfort, help, and the connection that comes from sharing someone's story. Fiction, nonfiction, sometimes poetry—all have spoken to me in troubled times.

Once, in deep despair, I came across a journal entry by short-story writer Katherine Mansfield. Her words, written to herself about her own suffering, comforted me greatly. I have sent them to others who are experiencing loss.

> There is no limit to human suffering. When one thinks: "Now I have touched the bottom of the sea—now I can go no deeper"—one goes deeper. There is no question of what is called "passing beyond it." One must submit. Do not resist. Take it. Be overwhelmed. Accept it fully. Make it part of life.

Everything in life that we really accept undergoes a change. So suffering must become Love.

Now I am like someone who has had her heart torn out—but—bear it—bear it. As in the physical world, so in the spiritual world, pain does not last forever. I will learn the lesson that suffering teaches. The fearful pain will fade . . . . Sorrow shall be changed into joy. Oh Life, accept me—make me worthy—teach me.

Often I murmured her final line as if it were a prayer.

a helping hand

Today you can easily find books or web sites about the difficulties of life, whether it's divorce, single parenting, elder care, job loss, a loved one's death, a pet's death, or (you fill in the blank).

Search for writers whose words speak to you. Wisdom words are never just for one reading, so copy their words into your journal or keep their books on your shelf. Like a shawl you pull on when cold, you can warm yourself with the right words again and again.

Mansfield's words helped me because her pain, too, was intense. As mine was! At the same time, she held on to hope, and her hope encouraged my own. By sharing her suffering, Katherine Mansfield helped me bear my own.

A Few Favorite Things

My son Andy was eighteen and in college when he sadly said to me, "Mom, I don't have any memories of my own about Daddy. I was too young when he died. Sometimes I'm jealous of my sister because she was older and remembers." He sighed. "I reach and reach, but I can never quite touch Daddy."

I stared at my son, aware for the first time of what a gift memory is.

What stirs *your* warm memories? Is it the big old leather chair beloved by your spouse? Or your mother's engagement ring? Or your granddad's chess set? Memorable objects bring a special kind of emotional support because they trigger special memories in us.

So many things reminded me of John in those first months after he died. His folk guitar, the baseball mitt he'd bought for his son, the colored slides from our camping trips, his half-finished, hand-painted duck decoys, even an old fishing lure. I held the fishing lure tight in both hands, brought it to my mouth, pressed my lips against it. I ran my fingers across the strings of his folk guitar.

One night, I took one of John's wool shirts to bed. The wool still smelled of him, and as I closed my eyes, I imagined he was next to me. I wrapped the shirt around me, letting it warm me, and for an instant— just an instant—I felt as if he might touch me, that his breath might blow in my ear.

a helping hand

After her little boy died, one grieving mother slept with her child's stuffed bear, the same bear that had hugged him to sleep at night. A few familiar things associated with someone you love can be very comforting.

Be aware, though, that in some losses, the opposite may be true. You may find comfort in *removing* an object from view, at least for a little while. Claire had to buy a new salad bowl. "It may sound silly," she told me, "but Charles made a big production of his

Caesar salad whenever we had company. After we separated, I started to cry every time I saw that salad bowl."

From Jolt to Joy

A woman who found her way to God through terrible loss is Joni Eareckson Tada. I read her book *Joni's Story* many years ago, and responded as I'm sure most readers did. I was horrified, saddened, then inspired. Joni Eareckson was eighteen when a dive into shallow water paralyzed her. Eventually fusion surgery gave her limited use of her upper arms, but nothing beyond that.

"My life had been so full," she wrote, "and now I was just a bare immobile body between two sheets. The beautiful horses in the barn which I used to trick ride—I would never ride them again. I couldn't even feed myself."

Joni couldn't reconcile her condition with her belief in a loving God. It took nearly three years of tears and violent questioning before she found a new way to connect.

"Gradually my focus changed from demanding an explanation from God to humbly depending on him. . . . I will never reach a place of self-sufficiency that crowds God out. I am aware of his grace every moment. . . ."

Eventually, Joni connected with millions of people through her writing, her artwork (which she accomplished with a brush held between her teeth), and her speaking. She also married, and her life became full again, though in a very different way from before.

I came across *Joni's Story* again as I was writing this book. I am still deeply moved by her willingness to believe in a loving God in the face of her loss.

In my own life, I once threw out a challenge to God. I was facing nothing as difficult as Joni Eareckson's paralysis, but I did have to make a tough decision that involved my children, and I was deeply troubled. My husband's death four years earlier had left a void where once I had experienced God. "Convince me you exist and you care!" I cried. I went to bed feeling as if I had thrown down a spiritual gauntlet.

Incredibly, when I woke up, something had shifted inside me. I had a warm, cared-for feeling, the kind you have when someone you love is standing beside you with a hand on your shoulder. For the first time in several years, I felt at peace, with a quiet certainty that I could make the right decision.

Abruptly, another thought intruded: Is this some psychological trick I'm playing on myself? Something felt different—new—inside me. Did the feeling come from God—or not? It occurred to me then that I had a choice.

I could believe. Or not believe.
I chose faith. I believed.
Joni Eareckson Tada chose to believe.
Faith is both a gift *and* a choice.

a helping hand

You can't wave a wand and magically have faith. "Faith is a sometimes win, sometimes lose struggle," wrote Antoinette Bosco in *Shaken Faith*. "When faith is firm, life makes sense. But when faith is elusive, we are like non-swimmers who have lost our water wings."

Faith becomes very elusive after a loss because life as you knew it ceases to exist. All you can do then is open yourself to trusting in something beyond you or deep within you to carry you through what comes next.

It's as simple—and as hard—as the first two steps in a Twelve-Step program, when (1) you acknowledge your own powerlessness and (2) state your willingness to believe that a power greater than yourself can restore some kind of meaning to your life.

"Our lives are not solely about us but about a power and a promise beyond us," wrote Antoinette Bosco. Joni Eareckson Tada's life had power beyond what was evident in her body. So perhaps faith is believing that your life has meaning even if you can't see it at this moment.

Here is a brief prayer that I like and often use: *"O Lord, I believe . . . please help my unbelief."*

Meditation in Motion

Meditation helped Sandy handle loss, though she came to it in a way she never expected. One autumn evening she was headed for her athletic club, just three blocks from her New York City apartment, when something heavy struck her from behind. She reeled from the impact. A hand—the fingernails short and grubby—yanked at her pursestrap, and a guttural voice snarled, "Give it to me, lady!" When Sandy tried to jump away, she was struck again. This time she fell. Something sticky and warm trickled into her eye. She blinked and yelled, but the man—a blur of old sneakers, denims, and nondescript shirt— had cut her purse strap and was running toward Central Park. She never saw him again.

The gash in her head required ten stitches, and for the first time, Sandy felt frightened about living in the city. She mourned her loss of a fear-free life. After a few weeks, she signed up for a martial arts course.

Sandy expected to study self-defense. She didn't expect her training to include a search for inner peace and harmony. But each class started and ended with the practice of meditation. Sandy learned how to breathe slowly, sit quietly in the silence, and maintain the kind of mental discipline that gradually led her to a sense of inner peace.

Eventually, she earned black belt status and regained her confidence in city living. But the real benefit of her training came when she suffered two major setbacks in her life. First, her twenty-year marriage foundered. Then she was diagnosed with cancer.

"I'm actually grateful for the mugging," she told me, "because without it, I might never have discovered martial arts, and through that, the practice of meditation. It's helped me feel peaceful despite my current problems."

a helping hand

It's not necessary to learn martial arts to practice meditation. Set aside twenty minutes in your day. Morning is best. Sit quietly in a chair or on a floor cushion. Begin taking slow, deep breaths. Focus on your breath until your thoughts—what I call my wriggling puppies—begin to settle down. You may choose to mentally repeat a holy word or "mantra." Common ones are "Peace" or "Praise God."

Observe the sensations in your body. Do your shoulders ache? Is there tension in your belly or your upper back? Your goal is not to change, but merely to notice how you feel. Have your thoughts rambled? It's okay. They will. When you notice, focus again on your breath or your holy word. Over time, regular meditation brings a calm, quiet ability to better handle life situations.

8.

Activities to Buoy You

I myself must mix with action
lest I wither by despair.

Alfred, Lord Tennyson

Just getting out of bed can seem hard when you're mourning a loss. You want to stay where you are and pull the covers over your head. I felt that way after John died, but one morning this thought occurred to me: "Other people have their own lives to live. If you persist in sitting in a corner and crying, Barb, eventually you'll sit in the corner alone."

It helped that I had kids who needed breakfast. Do you live alone? Then say out loud, "I can fake it 'til I make it" and get up and pour *yourself* a bowl of cereal.

Look for activities that speak to your soul.
Be open to trying something new.

One Step at a Time

October in Southern California has none of the autumn color of the Midwest. All I saw when I left my mom's house was the spiky green of palm trees. I was staying with my widowed mom while she fought a losing battle with cancer. Each day, as she weakened, my own spirits plummeted. I felt so helpless!

I began to walk for thirty minutes early in the mornings. I would follow the line of palm trees up the steep hilly street, relishing the pull on my calf muscles as I climbed. At the top of the hill, I had a panoramic view of the valley below. Then I meandered around and down other streets with manicured lawns and red-roofed stucco homes. As I walked, I often prayed out of my Christian tradition: "Jesus, have mercy. Christ, have mercy." The short prayers were like background music to other, more rambling thoughts.

The act of walking—the lift of knee, placement of foot, and swing of arms—was therapeutic. As the sun warmed my face, it reminded me that life—normal life beyond the sickroom—still went on. By the time I circled back to my mom's house, I always felt better.

a helping hand

It's when you least feel like exercising that you may benefit most. Exercise decreases the chance of grief merging into chemical depression.

If it seems too hard to do something vigorous, simply walk. Ten minutes in the morning. Ten minutes at night. My friend Joelle walked for long, solitary miles each day after her husband left her.

You, too, may prefer a solitary walk.

Or you might like company. It helps to walk a dog. It doesn't have to be your own dog; it could be a neighbor's. You might take a child or grandchild to the park and walk. One of the kindest things a friend can do is to offer to walk with you. If that doesn't happen, tell a friend that you'd like a walking buddy.

Something for You

Rachel went way beyond simple walking.

She was thirty-one when her husband Rod, also thirty-one, died of a brain aneurysm. Rachel couldn't believe it. They were both so health conscious! Why, they had met while jogging. Their dream was to compete one day in the grueling Ironman Triathalon in Hawaii, a swimming, bicycling, and running contest. Rod had run his usual eight miles just that morning. How could he be *dead*?

In the next six months so much about life seemed unfair. Rachel could hardly stand to see a pudgy coworker in his forties who smoked. "Why is he alive and not Rod?" she seethed. Every time their two-year-old daughter Gretchen asked for her daddy— "Daddy come home soon?"—Rachel felt as if her heart were breaking all over again.

Friends persuaded her to attend a widows' support group, but every woman there was at least twenty years older. *That's because you're not supposed to be a widow at thirty-one,* fumed Rachel. She left before the meeting ended. But one thing the speaker said stayed with her. "Do something that might seem selfish," urged the speaker. "Do something just for you."

A few nights later, as she studied her favorite photo of Rod, Rachel heard herself say, out loud, *"I'll compete in the Ironman."* The words hung in the air—startling, yet right. Here was an activity that could engage her physically and mentally, a goal that would help her heal.

For more than a year, she trained, even taking a three-month sabbatical from work. Her training paid off. In 1995, she became one of fifteen hundred contestants to compete in Hawaii in a 2.4 mile ocean swim, a 112-mile bicycle race, and a 26.2 mile run. In the final stretch, she felt as if somehow Rod ran beside her. She felt his presence, she said, because *"people may die, but love never does."*

a helping hand

"Out of order" deaths are the hardest kind to bear. A healthy young husband. A beloved younger sister. A child.

In untimely losses, anger is a normal part of grief. You may direct your anger at those you believe are responsible. A father whose young son was killed in a ski accident filed a lawsuit even though it was the father, according to witnesses, who had allowed his son to ski outside the safety perimeters. You may direct your anger at institutions. "I stopped going to church when I lost my eyesight," said Jennie, who suffers from macular degeneration. Or, like Rachel, you may feel anger at anyone not suffering as you are.

Anger is normal unless it turns into chronic resentment. Your spirit will suffer then as though an ulcer had eaten through your stomach. The bile you taste will be bitter, for resentment means *re-sentiment*, a re-experiencing of something painful. Like Sisyphus in Greek myth, a resentful person pushes a rock endlessly up the mountain, only to have it roll down again.

Rachel found a substitute for her anger in a goal that engaged her totally. What goal matters deeply to you? It may be a while before you're ready to answer that question, but open yourself to considering it. Beyond your grief may lie a new way of living your life.

Last summer, I watched a woman beach her bright yellow kayak on the shore of Lake Michigan. We started talking, and though I never did ask her name, she told me she had been a real workaholic until she was diagnosed with cancer. Losing her breast was a wake-up call. She began taking time to hike, camp, and kayak.

"Part of my healing process has been to recognize that I'm not running the show," she said. "In my kayak, I sit low and close to the water, and when I lift my paddle, it's as if I'm part of the boat, the water, the sky . . . the whole mystery of creation. I feel so grateful to be alive. Even without a breast, it seems natural to say thank you."

"Paddle prayer," I said.

She smiled. "That's a good name for it."

Healing Through Work

Jean Carnahan worked behind the scenes throughout her husband Mel's political career. When Mel, the Missouri governor who was running for senator, died in a plane crash in 2000, along with the Carnahan's oldest son, it was too close to the election to remove his name from the ballot. Supporters asked Jean to serve in his place should her husband win, and she agreed.

In an incredibly short period of time, Jean's life dramatically changed. She went from being a wife to being a widow and grieving mother to being a senator. Instead of talking politics at the dinner table, she began authoring national legislation.

When a third loss occurred that same year, and the Carnahan's family home burned to the ground, Jean dealt with it philosophically. Houses could be rebuilt, after all.

Her decision to serve in her husband's place had been a good one, Jean told reporters on the first anniversary of his death. She was glad to be championing causes her husband embraced and to be where she could make a difference.

Following the terrorist attacks on September 11, 2001, Senator Carnahan visited victims' families and rescue teams at the Pentagon. Speaking from her heart and her own experience, she said, "I have found that you get up in the morning and you do the thing you see as a duty, the immediate thing at hand. If you do that, it will become clearer what is the next thing to do.

"You live a day at a time, a step at a time. With the help of family, faith and friends, you are able to get through."

a helping hand

"People who do well after catastrophic change are those who can perceive the good in what is left of their lives," said Dr. Joseph Hyland, a psychiatrist I talked to in Topeka, Kansas.

Ask yourself: what in your life is still good?

◆ Commit to finding one good thing.

◆ You have lost your job. Do you have your health?

◆ You have lost your savings. Do you have usable skills?

◆ You have contracted a chronic disease. Do you have supportive friends? Is there hope through research?

◆ You have lost part of your hearing. Is your eyesight intact?

◆ Your knees gave way and you can no longer run. Can you bicycle?

◆ You have lost what you thought mattered most to you. Do you now find yourself turning to God in a new, deeper way?

God and "The Coneheads"

Jenny was a thirty-something mom, and already going through a difficult divorce, when she was diagnosed with breast cancer. It was too much. She needed God's help. "Oh God, let me hear your word," she prayed. Immediately, a word popped into her mind: *Conehead*.

Confused, Jenny prayed again. Again, came the thought: *Conehead*.

All right, God, is that your final answer?

So Jenny bought a flesh-covered conehead, like the ones made famous on the TV show *Saturday Night Live*. She wore it to her first chemotherapy session. The nurses smiled. So did the other patients.

Soon Jenny began devising more crazy costumes. An elephant's trunk. Antlers. A pig's snout. A Viking helmet. Once she went to her radiation treatment as the Cat in the Hat. Another time she put a tiara on her bald head and went as Queen Billiard at the Cue Ball. In all, she designed thirty-three different outfits.

Explained Jenny: "Humor was my weapon against pessimistic self-talk. It killed all the depressing thoughts in my mind."

Her zany humor helped keep her own fear at bay, and encouraged other patients too. One patient even rescheduled his appointments to match hers.

After two surgeries and dozens of radiation and chemo treatments, she was pronounced cancer-free. Now Jenny speaks to groups and is writing a book about how to use humor and faith against fear.

a helping hand

Jenny is not the first to use humor to help heal. Maybe you've read about Norman Cousins' groundbreaking use of humor to help in his fight against ankylosing spondylitis, a rare illness that doctors thought was fatal. His book *Anatomy of an Illness as Perceived by the Patient* eloquently describes how he moved out of the hospital into a nearby hotel room where, along with conventional medication, he took massive doses of vitamin C, and watched famous comics on film: Groucho Marx, Charlie Chaplin, W. C. Fields, Buster Keaton.

He discovered a good belly laugh eliminated his pain for an hour, and he credited humor with helping him achieve health again. He used humor differently than Jenny, not by becoming a purveyor, but by becoming a consumer of comedy. Many years later, he used the same techniques to help recover from a heart attack.

How can you help yourself with humor? By acting out, as Jenny did? Or by watching funny videos? Reading cartoon books? Playing with little children (whose laughter is infectious)?

Surround yourself with good-humored friends. Practice laughing.

A Greater Good

It's in doing something to help others that some ease their painful suffering.

Brenda Sewall had a hard time finding a doctor who would listen to her. But she persisted, and after years of pain and discomfort, was diagnosed with lupus. She created a web site to help others who had similarly struggled. On her home page she wrote, *"Don't let anyone tell you it's all in your head. Lupus is hard to diagnose and is different with each person."*

When Joanne Cacciatone's child died, she founded M.I.S.S. Foundation which has a web site titled *www.misschildren.org.* It's a place where parents can click and share their grief.

Candy Lightenen changed American attitudes and habits when she founded Mothers Against Drunk Driving after her daughter was killed by a drunken driver.

John Walsh successfully lobbied for national legislation to help other missing children after his son Adam was kidnapped and murdered.

Jim Kelly, a former Buffalo Bills quarterback, and his wife Jill started Hunter's Hope, a foundation to raise funds for the study of the deadly disease that afflicted their son Hunter.

These are just a few examples of how people have turned sorrow into action that, by benefiting others, helped them heal.

a helping hand

Not everyone feels called to become an activist. But at some point in your mourning process, it will be time to ask: "How do I give meaning to what has happened to me?"

During his internment in a World War II concentration camp, Jewish psychiatrist Viktor Frankl observed that prisoners who held on to their humanity, perhaps by the simple act of sharing a bread crust with another prisoner, were the ones most likely to survive. Later he wrote, "Despair is suffering without meaning."

You may begin your quest for meaning by courageously, quietly choosing to go on living. Children's author Andrea Warren, whose only son died when his bicycle was struck by a car, decided finally that what she could do was choose to stay sane. She didn't succumb to her paralyzing despair. She didn't become bitter. Painfully, but resolutely, she continued to live and continued to write. Her books bring history alive to readers who are the same age her son was when he died.

Boat Ride

For Jim, comfort came in the cold sea spray of Puget Sound. He turned his twenty-four-foot boat into the spray, relishing the hard thump as waves hit the boat's bottom. He glanced at his waterproof wristwatch. It was now . . . let's see . . . nineteen hours and ten minutes since the company had sent him packing. Not just him. Forty people in his department. The department itself was no more. *Doesn't say a damn thing about me,* he reminded himself. *Strictly a business decision. I'll get another job soon.*

But his gut twisted, and suddenly, he throttled up the boat's engine, jumping across the wake of a ferry. Sea gulls circled. A fish leaped. He took a deep breath, pulling the tangy air into his lungs. It helped put things in perspective to be out on the water. He cut the boat's engine, slowed a little. *It's not the end of the world*, he told himself. *I'll get another job.*

a helping hand

Going outdoors can be powerful therapy. A boat ride, a walk on the beach, a hike in the mountains. Gazing at a star-studded night sky. Nature's grandeur brings a sense of being part of something larger than yourself—and that brings a kind of peace, even in the midst of sorrow. It pulls you out of yourself and reminds you that you are not the center, but only a tiny part of a larger whole.

It's good to sense your connection with the universe and to realize that the same spirit flows through you and through water, snow, trees, rocks, sparrows. Such awareness doesn't remove your pain, but it may staunch it for a little while. As Jim Morris observed, it helps put things in perspective.

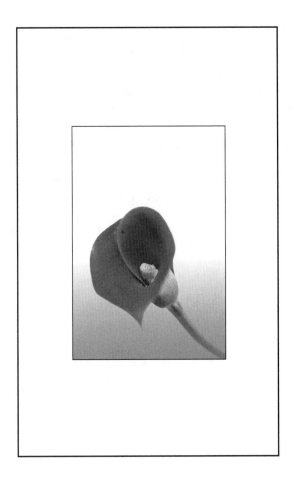

9.

$\mathcal{F}$acing Forward

---

*You could not step twice into the same river,
for other waters are ever flowing onto you.*

Heraclitus

fter any loss, you enter a new reality. Your life can never be exactly the same as it was before. Even if you were handed back your old job, even if your love affair rekindled, even if your home were rebuilt according to the same architectural plans, even then, would life be the same? How could it be? *You* would not be the same.

Buddhist teaching says the first fact of existence is the law of change or impermanence. Life is a process, a flow. The Bible uses different words to express the same idea: "For everything there is a season . . . a time to be born and a time to die. . . ." (Ecclesiastes 3:1-2).

It's not easy to traverse between what *was* and what *is*, and you have to transition at your own pace. The old pattern is not yet dissolved and the new not yet formed. Your mind may rebel and resist the change, leaving you feeling worse instead of better.

Accepting a new reality is seldom straightforward. Like a twig spiraling through the current of a river, you may glide ahead, then drift back. Over time, though, your momentum *is* forward, just as a river ultimately flows forward to the sea.

A favorite passage that has helped me is from T. S. Eliot's "Four Quartets":

> What we call the beginning is often the end
> And to make an end is to make a beginning.
> The end is where we start from.

"This is IT!"

Stuart's son Ben was born with spina bifida, a birth defect that strikes about one in every 1,000 newborns in the United States. The baby's spine fails to close properly during the mother's pregnancy, resulting in some degree of paralysis.

Many years later, Stuart told an audience, "I was ignorant at the time, so I thought if my son couldn't walk he would somehow be less than whole and probably ought not to live. It shames me to say that today. My thinking about 'wholeness' was wrong. It was too narrow."

Finally, he realized that you just have to cope, and the first tool of coping is to say, *"This is it!"*

Those three words became his family's credo. "No matter what else you would like to be doing, where else you would like to be, remind yourself, *this is it*. At this moment, you are right here, you are living with whatever is in front of you. You have no choice, so deal with it. Don't judge the moments you face as being good or bad, just let them be the moments of your life, then do what needs to be done."

Stuart remembers when his son faced his own *this is it!* moment. After long, arduous training, Ben had learned to walk with the aid of walking sticks. But one wintry day, six-year-old Ben's walking stick slipped on some melted snow inside a store entry. He went down. *Hard!* People rushed to help, but Ben's father quietly stopped them. "Ben needs to get up by himself," he said. It was painful to watch his son struggle, but finally Ben pulled himself upright.

"It was Ben's moment," said Stuart, with pride in his voice. "He had to deal with a tough situation, and he did. It made him stronger. More independent." Stuart became stronger too. He joined his state's Spina Bifida Association, eventually becoming president, and he and his wife adopted a child born with the same defects as their son's.

a helping hand

Even saying the words *This is it!* may bring tears to your eyes. Part of you may want to scream, "No! This can't be it! I don't want it to be!" Of course you don't. No one other than a masochist willingly chooses pain. But part of moving on is to squarely face your reality, and the paradox is that when you do, you're better able to bear it. Ride your pain as a surfer rides a wave.

Suffering has been defined as that space between desire and acceptance. Once you accept what is, you'll discover a change of energy in mind and body—a supple strength you didn't know you had. Some call it the strengthening power of God's grace.

Can you accept—just for today—that *"This is it"*?
Can you surrender what *you* want and make the best
of what you have? Try it. Just for today, ride the
wave.

Mournful Voices

It was hard for me to accept my new reality after
John died. A continuous mournful voice seemed to
thread itself through my mind: "Somebody love
me . . . somebody love me."

I appeared to function independently, but inside,
I still felt only half-whole. I craved to be loved again.
I wanted to be someone's wife. I wanted a partner to
love and take care of me and make me feel whole.

When I started dating, I continually wondered,
"Are you the one? The one who will love and marry
me? Who will rescue me from this terrible desert of
total responsibility?"

After two years, I thought I had found him. My
fiancé was a young professor with a Harvard Ph.D.
whom I'd met in graduate school. He got along well
with my three children, and when he asked me to
marry him, I happily said yes. I liked knowing that
once we were married, I'd become part of the academic world, just as earlier I'd been part of the
Navy world.

But six weeks before our wedding, my fiancé
begged off. He wasn't ready, after all, for the responsibility of a ready-made family. I screamed at him,
and then I screamed at God, *"How can you take this
from me when I dared to love again?"*

Now I want to both laugh and cry as I look back
at the young woman I was. Now, I say in thanksgiving: *Thank you, God*. I wasn't any more ready to get
married than the professor. I was trying to escape
into the false security of another special world—

academic this time instead of military. An egoistic part of me had even managed to replace the prestigious Naval Academy husband with an equally prestigious Harvard spouse.

The tough work of growing was tiring, and I thought marriage would let me relax. It was years before I realized what a difference there is between wanting to *be* loved and growing into the maturity *to* love.

a helping hand

Anyone who yearns to be rescued from the hard task of growing and moving forward should pick up the book *The Missing Piece Meets the Big O* by children's author Shel Silverstein. It begins with these words:

> The missing piece sat alone
> waiting for someone
> to come along
> and take it somewhere. . . .

In the simplest of drawings and with the profoundest of meanings, Silverstein says you're not ready for a relationship when you feel less than whole (like a missing piece). First become complete in yourself (like the big O).

Becoming a whole person is a lifetime journey. There is so much to it. But you can start by knowing yourself a little better. Think about the answers to these questions:

◆ If you absolutely, positively knew you could not fail, what would you do and who would you be?

◆ How would you like to be remembered? (What would you like your obituary to say?)

◆ Are you living in a way that moves you toward who you want to be, what you want to do, and how you want to be remembered after you're gone? If not, what is one thing you can do in the next thirty days?

Choosing the Attitude

Robin, a high school cheerleader, always had *attitude*. Why, it even said so on her car license plate: *ATI2D*.

When one of Robin's knees began to stiffen, she thought it was a pulled muscle. Then x-rays and further tests at the Mayo Clinic confirmed the worst. Robin had osteosarcoma, a bone cancer that afflicts teenagers. Surgery removed the tumor but left her with a prosthetic knee, and chemotherapy made her nauseous for weeks at a time. She was rushed, over and over, to the hospital's intensive care unit. The risk of catching a cold or developing a fever made it impossible to continue going to school.

"This can't be real," Robin thought. "This isn't really happening to me."

But it was happening. And finally, she dealt with her new reality just as she had dealt with her life in happier times. She adopted an *attitude*. Cancer wouldn't beat her! When she couldn't attend classes, she studied at home between bouts of nausea. When her hair fell out, she shaved her head and went as Mr. Clean to a Halloween party.

Robin chose to face her situation in a combative, upbeat way. Because of her tenacity in keeping up with schoolwork, she was able to graduate with her classmates. Her walk across stage felt triumphant, even though she had to use a cane.

a helping hand

You can't always choose what happens to you, but you can choose your response. David Burns, M.D., a pioneer in cognitive research, has studied the way changing your thoughts can change emotions and the ability to solve problems or rally from difficulties. Pay attention to how you think. Stay alert for distortions such as "never" ("I'll never get better!") or "always" ("I *always* blow it!"). Avoid either/or thinking ("Either I do it perfectly or I'm a total failure."). Consider reframing your situation. ("Losing my job isn't what I planned, but it gives me the chance to start my own business.") Reframing doesn't deny the facts; it just changes how you interpret them.

Members of AA put it this way: if you want to move forward in a positive manner, "stop your stinkin' thinkin'!"

Lost and Found

There are many ways to reframe a situation. I listened to Laurie, a freelance artist, explain her move to the small seaside town where her best friend Judy lived. She and her grown daughter had become alienated, and their estrangement made Laurie very sad. She hoped it might help to relocate. Start a new life.

Sure enough, Laurie loved her new location. She could hear seals bark offshore as she gardened. All that the town lacked, she observed to Judy, was an artsy café where writers, artists, and others could hang out. "Let's open a café!" said Judy. "Okay," said Laurie.

They used an inheritance of Laurie's for seed money and agreed to be 50-50 partners. But their views of running a café were very different. Squabbles turned into divisive quarrels over money and time. After a year, the business folded, and so did their friendship.

Divorce from a best friend is nearly as painful as divorce from a spouse. For a long time, Laurie sat slumped inside her tiny seaside house, grieving. She couldn't work or even think clearly. Then one day, she walked outside and the air held a tang. A breeze lifted her hair. She heard the seals bark, and as she looked around her small garden, she felt as if she were waking up from a dream. Life wasn't turning out as she'd expected, but the sun was shining, and— *"Hey, here I am!"* She decided she'd make the best of it. (Can you hear echoes of *"This is it"*?)

Laurie began taking small steps. Filling out the bankruptcy forms. Weeding her garden. Inviting several women she'd met to lunch.

What happened next was totally unexpected. Laurie's daughter called. Newly divorced and with a small child, she wanted to reconcile and move closer to her mother. "It was like a miracle," said Laurie, adding ruefully, "I lost my best friend and regained my daughter. Go figure.

"This has taught me that you can plan all you want," she added. "But in the end, life will surprise you. So stay flexible. Go with the flow. And be open to surprise."

a helping hand

Easier to say than to do, but one way to start is by focusing on your life at this exact moment. What do you smell? Fresh-brewed coffee? New-mown grass? What do you hear? The chirp of birds waking? Your baby's laugh? What do you feel in your body? What do you see around you? Stop reading for a moment and observe.

When you live in the moment, you are living more consciously. A French priest in the nineteenth century coined the phrase "the *sacrament* of the present moment." A sacrament is merely an outward sign of an inward grace. By paying attention to what's happening *now*, you're more likely to recognize the miracle of grace.

There's a wonderful quote from writer Don Campbell, "When you walk with God be prepared to find surprises along the way." Yes. Appreciate this moment. And, as you do, open yourself to appreciating all of Life's giddy surprises.

Called to Action

The headline said, *Man Freed from Wrongful Imprisonment*. As I read the news story, I tried to imagine Dennis's reality. What was it like to be imprisoned for life for a rape and murder you knew you had not committed? To be innocent yet labeled one of society's worst kinds of felons? To feel betrayed by the judicial process? To feel helplessly, unfairly ensnared?

"You carry around bitter feelings," Dennis acknowledged. "If you're guilty, you can feel remorse and begin healing, but it's different when you're innocent. Your emotions are harder [to handle] than the actual prison life."

The way Dennis coped was through action. He spent hundreds of hours in the prison law library working on his case. Despite setbacks, he refused to quit, and eventually, his diligence paid off. In 1999, after fourteen years of incarceration, he proved his innocence through the new tool of DNA testing.

Fourteen years lost, I thought, marveling.

When he was first freed, Dennis appeared on many TV news and talk shows to push for state-mandated DNA testing for prisoners. Going public on the issue helped him give some meaning to his own lost years.

a helping hand

You probably aren't worried about going to prison. But certain kinds of losses do seem rampantly unfair, and carry with them a sense of being wrongly accused. You may feel your reputation was smirched by the way your company let you go, or you're humiliated by the way your ex-spouse ended your marriage. Constant criticism also brings a feeling of unfair accusation, making old tapes flare—those half-remembered accusations by parents or teachers when you were a kid.

It's tempting to hold on to righteous anger. But that can lead to a prison of a different sort, one of your own making. The apostle Paul, who faced more than his share of accusations, warned, "Get rid of all bitterness, anger, and rage." Get rid of it for your own sake, before it consumes you in its fire.

If you're feeling unfairly accused, clarify to yourself what the circumstances are. Then list constructive steps to either remedy your situation or to just let it go.

Letting go is not a one-time process. To help, consider using something as a touchstone. A friend gave me a rosary ring after I separated from my second husband. It fit on my pinkie finger and had ten bumps on it, symbolizing prayer beads. Whenever I got pulled in by bitter thoughts, I yanked off the ring and started praying. Soon, my mind would quietly refocus. You could even use your own body. *"When I touch my forehead, I'll stop these destructive thoughts."*

Ages and Stages

Not all losses are as dramatic as Dennis's. Some may not even be viewed as losses by others, which can leave you feeling guilty or doubting your own feelings.

When my daughter Allison left for college, she got very upset when I said I might turn her bedroom into a study. "Don't touch my room!" she said. "I want it to be here for me when I come home."

She reminded me of a little bird learning to fly. As eager as she was to be on her own, part of her clung to childhood, and wanted to keep her place in the nest. So I left her room alone, and it stayed as it had been, with her high school bedspread on the bed, her stuffed animals on the shelves, and her posters on the wall. All were waiting for her, even though she was soon so busy with college that she seldom came home except for a few weeks each summer.

Finally, during Christmas break of her senior year, she said, almost casually, "Oh, Mom, if you want to use my room for something else, go ahead."

I hid a smile. The reality was, she had moved on long ago. It just took her a while to recognize it.

a helping hand

Even when it's a positive change, you leave something behind. I call such losses "little griefs." They're not major, like death or divorce or losing all your savings, but they're not to be ignored, either. Little griefs require less effort and time, but they include the same stages as larger bereavements.

It may be hard for you to leave a comfort zone. Perhaps you've always needed more structure. Your life experience makes a difference too. If you moved frequently while growing up, a move won't frighten you the way it would if you'd spent your whole life in one small town.

Sometimes accumulated small events reach the stress level of a single, larger event. Doctors Thomas Holmes and Richard Rahe worked out a point system to record the impact of various life events on a person, ranging from 100 points for the death of a spouse to 11 points for a traffic violation. Suppose you get married, acquire a stepchild, start a new job, and watch a parent die, all within six months. Those add up to a lot of points!

You can't move on from something never acknowledged, so give yourself permission to recognize little griefs. Let yourself be sad for a while. One friend chuckled, "I sat and cried and cried, until after awhile, I got bored with crying."

That's when you're ready to take a breath and move on.

Be Not Afraid

Moving forward can bring peace, and often is marked by a deepened faith. Sometimes it includes a willingness to surrender *all*. Even life itself.

Kathy sat in her wheelchair facing those who crowded into the small chapel. Though not yet fifty-five, she was terminally ill with a brain tumor. Kathy had invited students and friends to join her at Mass so she could say thank-you. "I've never known so much love and caring," she said to the crowd of well-wishers.

But the others saw it as their chance to thank *her*.

For years, Kathy, a popular dance instructor, had turned her students into performers, if only for an evening. She awakened in many a new awareness of themselves as poised, talented young people. In the chapel, they laughed as Kathy parodied her well-known discipline. "You *can* belly dance," she said from her wheelchair. Then, in a German taskmaster's voice, she added: "You *vill* belly dance!"

Kathy knew her life was ending. She had gone through the stages of being sad, wanting to fight, being scared, until, in the end, she surrendered to what she could not change. "Then she led the rest of us through the final stage of acceptance," said her friend Judy.

It's a special gift when someone can show others how to live—*and*, when life is ending, how to die. Like Kathy, my friend Don gathered in front of a large group of friends just two weeks before he died of colon cancer.

His six-foot frame was gaunt. He barely weighed a hundred pounds. But with his familiar lopsided grin, Don quoted one of his favorite scriptures: "Shoulder my yoke and learn from me. . . My yoke is easy and my burden light." (Matthew 11:29-30 NJB). Shrugging his skinny shoulders, he said, "I feel as though every night since my surgery, Jesus has reshaped his yoke to fit my shrinking shoulders. So it's still not too heavy. And I'm not afraid. The end of one life is the beginning of another."

a helping hand

Fans of the *Beatles* mourned George Harrison when he died. Yet the "quiet Beatle" held such a deep faith in life after death, it seemed appropriate for a

ιe story to end with these words: ". . . he
d to let go." Nor, at the end, were Kathy

ally, the willingness to acknowledge
your own mortality may enhance your love of life.
The terrorism of September 11, 2001, aroused in many
people a heightened appreciation for life's gifts: for
their loved ones, for the beauty in nature, for their
own health, for a country that believes in freedom.

Life is a series of repeated endings and letting go.
Can you summon the faith to stop clutching at your
past? Can you release your expectations of what your
life "should" be? Can you read and believe the words
of T. S. Eliot: "To make an end is to make a beginning.
The end is where we start from"?

Broken Glass

In the early months after my husband John died,
I continually yearned for all I'd lost. One morning, as
I fixed breakfast for the kids, a juice glass fell and
shattered on the kitchen floor. I stared at the broken
fragments and burst into tears. *My life is like this glass*,
I thought, *shattered into pieces*. Then, a startling image
popped into my mind—a picture of our church's
stained-glass window. Wasn't it made of pieces of
broken glass? The image surprised me and brought a
healing insight. For the first time since my loss, I realized I could create a new reality out of the shattered
pieces of my life. It wouldn't be the same as the one
John and I had shared, but it could still be beautiful.

a helping hand

If your life, too, seems shattered, sit quietly and visualize the pieces taking shape as a new picture. Maybe you can't fit all the pieces together just yet, but can you see an outline? You can't have your old picture, but what will make your new reality an image you can cherish? Does it require a new definition of who you are? The healing of a broken relationship? A new place to live?

Are you clinging to the picture your parents drew for you when you were a child? Or the one created by religious or societal rules? Or did you construct a picture at age twenty-one, and never reexamined it? You're reading this book because you're going through a loss, which means you are now adapting to a new reality.

Each day sit for a few moments, close your eyes, and try to see your new picture. In time, it will become clear, and the pieces will fit together. Be patient with yourself. As poet Robert Frost said, sometimes you have to "get lost *enough* to find yourself."

10.

Transformation

*It appears that when life is broken by tragedy
God shines through the breach.*

George A. Buttrick

*L*oss has the power to transform. And to be transformed is to be changed.

In coping with your loss, you stretch, expand, and become more than you otherwise might have been. After losing a job, you find the courage to learn a new skill. After betrayal, you focus on eventual forgiveness instead of retribution. After divorce, you discover new capabilities and a new life. If your loss is physical decline or a natural departure of youth, you waste no time on regrets, but look for the gifts in what remains.

The apostle Paul said, "All things work for good to those who love God." He didn't say loss itself is good. What could possibly be good about a child's death or a senseless murder? But in time, through the way you respond, suffering can transform you—and others—in ways that lead to good.

But no one can do it alone. Like Paul, I believe transformation happens with the help of God's grace.

And one way to open yourself to God's grace is through *prayer*.

Don't think you haven't prayed just because you haven't used formal prayer. I've known people whose prayer was not so much specific words as the attitude they adopted. Despite their loss—or, momentarily, their despair—they stayed open to seeing life's ultimate goodness. And by the way they chose to see, they found light again.

God's grace works like the sun on a cloudy day. Even when you can't see it, its fiery energy keeps the earth alive. Looking back, I see how grace worked in my life even when my own myopia threw up a cloud cover. God was there when my prayers retreated far from conscious words.

It isn't so for everyone. Some people get stuck in their sorrow or resentment or anger. It's as if their emotions build a high stone wall that completely surrounds them. They can't see out or scale their wall or walk around it. So they live behind it, missing the beauty of budding trees, the laugh of a child, the warming touch of a caress.

In coping with the losses that have threaded my life, I've come to trust in God's grace. Now I know it's there for me with the same certainty that I know there are stars in the sky. The *knowing* hasn't come easily, but it has come. And it can come to you too.

New Life

On January 9, 2002, four months after her husband died, Lisa Beamer gave birth to a baby girl. Todd Beamer, thirty-two, was the one who cried, "Let's roll!" as he and fellow passengers prepared to fight the terrorists who had captured their plane on September 11. Their efforts brought the plane down in a Pennsylvania field. All forty-four aboard were killed, but they prevented their hijacked aircraft from hitting the White House or another major landmark in Washington, D.C.

Though Lisa lost Todd, she told reporters later, "Some people live their whole lives, long lives, without having left anything behind. My children will be told their whole lives that their father was a hero, that he saved lives. It's a great legacy for a father to leave his children."

a helping hand

As a child, I remember hearing the phrase "the mark of the cross." It had to do with the belief that the pain and suffering of crucifixion were transformed into a mark of love, hope, and forgiveness. In the most tangible way possible, Lisa Beamer's baby girl transformed a horrific act into resurrected love and hope. It's the love a mother feels for her child and the hope that is in every new life.

What has been birthed in your life through your response to your loss? What strengths or talents? What have you learned about yourself? What patterns have you changed that caused you trouble in the past? What networks of friends have you built? What dreams have you pulled out of hiding? How has your spiritual life deepened?

Spend some quiet time pondering your answers to these questions and any others that come to mind. Acknowledge your own growth and achievements. Do it in writing so you have a memento you can reread. It's good to remind yourself how far you have come.

One morning over coffee with three women friends, we shared our stories of loss and growth. I looked around the table and marveled. One friend, left with four children and no college education, was now the executive assistant to the CEO of a major medical center. Another watched her husband walk out on her six weeks after she was diagnosed with cancer. She beat the cancer, went back to school, and became director of a community mental health center. Another, widowed and then divorced from a second husband, took up sculpting at the age of fifty-five, and would soon have her first showing. "I'm in awe of what we've done," she said. "*How did we do it?*"

I think we had the help of grace. Grace, like electricity, is there to be used. The four of us apparently plugged in.

How have you tapped into that powerful force?

Knowing Yourself

Shortly after my daughter married, she said to her new husband, "Please telephone if you're coming home late from work. I assume the worst. I don't stop at 'beer with the guys' or 'flat tire' or 'late meeting with the boss.' I go from late to *death*."

My otherwise level-headed daughter knew her anxiety was irrational. It was a holdover from childhood when the worst she could imagine *did* happen. Her father died. Now, as an adult, she needed reassurance from her own imagined scenarios.

She laughed at her fears, but she still wanted that phone call!

We do feel more vulnerable after a loss. It shows us that we're not always in control, and that bad things can happen to good people. They can happen to *us*.

But also out of coping with her childhood grief, my daughter was transformed into a woman who knows and accepts herself. Her own self-knowledge makes her very empathetic of others. Friends comment on her willingness to listen without judging. She has a wisdom about life that I didn't possess until I was twice her age.

a helping hand

To realize you are vulnerable and mortal is not a bad thing. It reduces the ego, helps you keep "first things first," and makes you more willing to turn to God. It lessens your compulsion to judge and can help you respond more caringly to others. Laugh a little at your anxieties and remember what the Psalmist says: "The Lord is my light and my salvation. Whom shall I fear?"

Gifts of a Lifetime

"Happy birthday, Grandpa!" With a warm hug, my grown son John bent toward his grandpa's wheelchair. I followed them into the nursing home's social room. Red, yellow, and blue balloons floated near the ceiling. A large cake spelled out in blue frosted letters: *Happy 100th Birthday*. It was a happy occasion, but I felt oddly unsettled.

"You're looking good, Grandpa!" shouted my other son Andy, close to Grandpa's ear. Grandpa beamed. He reached out a trembling hand, and Andy clasped it.

The room grew noisy as other family and friends streamed in. My daughter Allison called, "Mom, will you get Grandpa's shawl? He's chilly."

I slipped out to Grandpa's room. It smelled of camphor and Vicks, the subtle traces left by the very, very old. A framed photo sat on his bedside table and I picked it up. It was my deceased husband John in his naval uniform.

John's father has lived sixty-six years longer than his son, I thought. *Another whole lifespan.*

"You died too young," I murmured. I felt John's absence like a hole in Grandpa's birthday cake.

When I returned to the party, someone called, "Time to sing." My son John picked up his guitar, the guitar that had belonged to his father. I heard in his voice an echo of his dad's clear tenor as he led us in singing, "Happy Birthday."

As Grandpa blew out the birthday candles, my children laughed and kidded with their three grown cousins. I caught a glimpse of Andy's profile. Andy had inherited his father's keen mind for science, just as John had his dad's musical talent, and Allison, her father's tenderness.

I looked at our family—our warm, extended family—and suddenly, I noticed what I had failed to see before. My husband died young, and his children missed out on their father's living presence. But through family stories and pictures, through inherited traits, and in the loving connections that had drawn us together this day, he had still influenced their lives.

A quote floated into my mind, something from some long ago English Lit class. *"He who is remembered is not dead."* My son Andy clasped my hand. "It's been a good day, hasn't it, Mom?" My daughter called, "Smile, everyone!" Cameras clicked. I touched Grandpa's shoulder. I felt John's presence. "A very good day," I replied.

a helping hand

When someone you love dies "too young," grief may be compounded because you feel as if so much potential was lost.

Similar feelings can occur to someone diagnosed with MS at age thirty. Or to someone who loses a job that was supposed to be a steppingstone. Or to someone whose financial investment goes awry, losing money meant to fund a dream.

Part of transforming grief into joy includes a willingness to surrender *your* ideas of what life should be like. Instead, embrace the simple (though not easy) belief that if you live and work in concert with God, ultimately all will be well. Not as you may have planned it, but all will be well.

Theologian Mary Hynes, Ph.D., wrote this:

> Surrender, most simply put, is living out of the recognition that we are not God. It's not an excuse for apathy or irresponsibility. It means recognizing we are not the ultimate power. We must do what we can and allow God to do the rest.

Once you've done all you can, can you let go? Can you be more accepting of your life as it is, and not live in the past? In her book *Surrender*, Dr. Hynes suggests this small daily exercise. Clench your hands into tight fists. Then slowly, prayerfully open them. As you do, open yourself to accepting what cannot be changed, and to living in gratitude for the gifts that remain.

Transformational Strength

The list is long of public figures who were transformed by loss.

It was after Eleanor Roosevelt discovered her husband was having an affair with one of her trusted friends that she began taking the steps that made her a powerful voice for women and the downtrodden everywhere.

It was after Gandhi experienced the searing humiliation of racial prejudice in South Africa that he began his efforts to free India of British rule through nonviolent means.

It was after Katherine Graham's husband committed suicide that the shy, retiring homemaker became one of America's most powerful and admired newspaper publishers.

It was after his own stroke that actor Kirk Douglas began encouraging other stroke patients to learn new communication skills as a way to overcome depression.

It was after John Walsh lost his six-year-old son Adam in a terrible abduction and murder that he began working to reform laws regarding missing children. The Fox TV show *America's Most Wanted*, which Walsh hosts, not only increased public awareness, but is credited with leading to the capture of four hundred fugitives.

In an interview on Larry King's show, Walsh talked with satisfaction about the number of murderers caught through response to the show. His face lit up as he expressed the joy he felt when an abducted child was returned home. But he also said that the pain of losing a child stays with you forever. What you can do is transform your pain by using it to serve others.

a helping hand

A quiet satisfaction comes when you help another, a sense that you are living God's command to love your neighbor. Noted writer Henri Nouwen coined the phrase "the wounded healer." Who can better heal another than someone who's been similarly wounded?

Let yourself appreciate how you have been of service, in small and large ways. A widow I spoke to described how she started leading bereavement groups. A Colorado man who loves to ski volunteered to guide blind skiers. It helped him pull out of a depression after his divorce. A friend whose parent has Alzheimer's disease happened to sit next to someone on a recent plane flight whose wife has Alzheimer's disease. She told me later, "We spent the entire flight talking. He helped me so much. I got off the plane feeling encouraged."

And perhaps you serve without even knowing it. A woman in my church has two disabled children. The children's father, unable to handle the stress, left his family, so she copes alone. Every Sunday I watch her push her son's wheelchair up the aisle. Her expression of love as she holds his palsied hand never fails to move me. She models a calm, loving courage.

Think about ways in which you, too, have modeled courage.

Perspective

In chapter two, I told the story of Gary, Donna, and John, a Missouri farm family who experienced the pain of bankruptcy. Something happened to the family that transformed the way Donna viewed their farm sale.

One afternoon a few weeks after the sale, Donna's son John complained of a funny pressure in his chest. His pulse was racing and his heart had gone into an odd rhythm. Frightened, Donna bundled him into their pick-up and raced toward the hospital. As she drove, she began to pray, "Oh, God, I'm willing to lose our farm. And everything we possess. But please, save our child!"

She waited tensely while doctors ran tests. Finally, the report came. John had a mitral-valve prolapse. It was serious, but with medication, he would be fine.

Donna slumped in her chair, weak with relief. And suddenly, she saw life with a vibrant new clarity. "I saw how abundantly I have lived. It has nothing to do with money or the farm. Abundance is in the sunset, or the smell of hay, or my garden in spring. It's in the laughter—and in the *lives*—of my two boys. And I realized it's all on loan. I'm not *entitled* to any of it. My son is not mine. My husband is not mine. I can only be thankful for all that I have."

Donna's outlook on life was transformed from one of anger and resentment into quiet gratitude. The family's financial problems didn't disappear, but she saw them now in a larger context. She saw how much she had, not how much she had lost.

a helping hand

Transformation calls for a new way of seeing. Your perception acts as a filter, so you quite literally see only what you expect to see. Once your vision enlarges, you notice what was always there but what you failed to discern before. You see blessings as well as losses. It's not that your loss becomes less, but that you see beyond it.

All religious traditions support this. Mahatma Gandhi, when asked to describe his life, smilingly replied, "Renounce—and enjoy." He quoted from the Hindu *Upinishad*: "The whole world is the garment of the Lord. Renounce it, then, and receive it back as the gift of God."

Similar expressions are found in the Old and New Testaments. Job, after all his sufferings, still renounced guilt and anger, and continued to acknowledge the sovereignty of God. In consequence, ". . . the Lord made him prosperous again [with] twice as much as he had before."

Jesus advised, "Strive first for the kingdom of God and his righteousness, and all these things will be given to you as well" (Matt 6: 33). And Isaiah said so beautifully, "but those who wait for the Lord shall renew their strength, they shall mount up with wings like eagles, they shall run and not be weary, they shall walk and not faint" (40:31).

Losing a job or a farm or anything you counted on is painful. It is right to mourn. It is also right to remember the wisdom of scripture, and eventually stop clinging to what is past.

Is it time to begin counting your blessings? Go back mentally through your last few days and recall some of life's small joys. A friend calls these her "domestic miracles." The crayoned drawing of your little daughter, held out to you with a beaming smile. A rose, newly blossomed, in your garden. The loving phone call from a friend.

Another friend, with a chuckly sense of humor, said she wakes up each morning, looks around, and says, "Oh goody! I got another one!" Yes! Rejoice and be glad! It's a new day.

Contentment

It was the third week of January, the time of year when we're still resolved to eat less, save more, and exercise better. "You know something?" said my friend Jim. "I'm not praying as much as I used to. And I haven't written in my journal in a long time."

"I know why. It's because you're happier."

"You think?"

I laughed. We were sitting in front of the fire, ready to begin our weekly *Scrabble* game. A bowl of popcorn sat on the table. My little dog Sandy was curled up near my feet. The room held an ambiance of warm contentment. Life felt good.

It hadn't felt so good when Jim and I met four years earlier. We were both emerging from mid-life divorces. Over get-acquainted coffee, we talked about the sadness of being middle aged and knowing that the spouse you planned to be a grandparent with had now found another partner.

Jim told me then that he was keeping a journal. He'd held up a large, blank-page book, neatly filled in with his careful penmanship. It was something new for him. And for the first time in his life, he was trying to spend thirty minutes a day in quiet prayer.

"I've always liked church," he said, "but this meditation stuff—it's hard."

I'd been starting my days with an hour of prayer and spiritual reading for about fifteen years, but I remembered how scary it had felt in the beginning. No ritual. No pastor. No group prayer. Just me—and God.

"Keep it up," I urged Jim. "It will make a difference."

A few weeks later, we had a movie date. Then I came down with the flu, and Jim fixed me homemade chicken soup. I was touched. No one had ever fixed me homemade soup before.

We began taking walks together. I noticed I was laughing more. We started meeting for church on Sundays. Jim brought over his *Scrabble* game and left it. In the spring, he planted flowers for me in my garden.

Now, as he got up to stir the fire, I repeated, "Yep. People are more inclined to journal and pray when they feel bad. It's as if we bottle God like aspirin to keep on the shelf for emergencies only."

Jim grew quiet. So did I.

I was thinking about my own prayer life, and how my view of God had changed. "I pray God to let go of God," wrote the twelfth-century mystic Meister Eckart. His words puzzled me until I realized that growing spiritually means gradually altering your view of God.

In my twenties, God was definitely aspirin. For a long while after my husband John died, God became an existential void.

Little by little, I stopped thinking of God as aspirin. Or a kind of fairy godfather who would grant me all my wishes. Or an existential void. Or a bearded judge ready to stomp on me for my transgressions.

Gradually, I began to have a different view. It was a life-encompassing view in which God, not I, lived at the center. I stopped getting angry when life didn't happen exactly as I expected. My losses became, instead of punishments, a natural weaving of joy and sorrow.

I saw that I could help design my life by the responses I chose. And I could trust God. If I surrendered my will to the loving will of God, then I could be assured that whatever happened in life, I would find the grace I needed to comfort and strengthen me.

These thoughts tumbled through my mind faster than I am writing them here.

The fire leaped, and Jim reached over and clasped my hand. "I *am* happy," he said. "And you're right. I talked to God a lot when I was in despair. I need to get back into regular prayer—only this time in thanksgiving."

"Gratitude is good," I said. We smiled at each other and started our *Scrabble* game.

a helping hand

In Elisabeth Kübler-Ross's five stages of grief, the final stage is *acceptance*. But this doesn't mean a cringing, tail-between-the-legs resignation. It means opening your fists and releasing your defiant hold on life as you want it to be, or life as you think it should be. Acknowledge, finally, the reality of your life *now*.

You would not have chosen this cup, but here it is, so drink of it, go into it, feel it, open your arms to it, and willingly learn all it can teach you.

And pray.

The great psychologist Carl Jung wrote, "People from all civilized countries have consulted me, and . . . none has really been healed who did not regain his religious outlook." Jung didn't mean a set of doctrines, but a way of *seeing*.

All life is a series of endings and new beginnings.

Winter's fossiled limbs stretch skyward before April's buoyant resurrection.

Every life includes loss. It's not that all losses are inevitable or should have happened. Some are patently unfair. Some we bring on ourselves. What is natural is life's intermingling of joy and sorrow, sun and shade.

To rediscover joy, rediscover God.
Start right now. Where you are.
Your prayer can be as simple as "Oh, God."
God will take it from there.

Resources

Anatomy of an Illness as Perceived by the Patient by Norman Cousins. New York, 1991: Bantam, Doubleday, Dell.

Crazy Time: Surviving Divorce and Building a New Life by Abigail Tafford. New York, 1982: HarperPerennial.

The Dance of Anger by Harriet Goldhor Lerner, Ph.D. New York, 1985: Harper & Row.

Feeling Good: The New Mood Therapy by David D. Burns, M.D. New York, 1980: William Morrow and Company.

Four Quartets by T. S. Eliot. New York, 1974: Harvest/HBJ Book.

Healing Words: The Power of Prayer and the Practice of Medicine, by Larry Dossey, M.D. New York, 1993: HarperCollins.

Invitation to a Great Experiment: How to Start a New Way of Life That Works by Thomas E. Powers. East Ridge, NY, 1986: East Ridge Press.

Joni's Story by Joni Earekson Tada. Grand Rapids, MI, 1976: Zondervan Publishing.

Man's Search for Meaning by Viktor Frankl. New York, 1963: Washington Square Press/Simon & Schuster.

The Missing Piece Meets the Big O by Shel Silverstein. New York, 1981: HarperCollins Juvenile Books.

The Mourning Handbook by Helen Fitzgerald. New York, 1994: Simon & Schuster.

Necessary Losses by Judith Viorst. New York, 1986: Simon & Schuster (Fireside Books).

New Seeds of Contemplation, by Thomas Merton. New York, 1961: New Directions Publishing Corporation.

Nobody's Child Anymore: Grieving, Caring, and Comforting When Parents Die by Barbara Bartocci. Notre Dame, IN, 2000: Sorin Books.

Prayers for a Planetary Pilgrim: A Personal Manual for Prayer and Ritual by Edward Hayes. Leavenworth, KS, 1989: Forest of Peace Publishing.

Rilke's Book of Hours: Love Poems to God by Rainer Maria Rilke, Joanna R. Macy (contributor), Anita Burrows (translator). New York, 1997: Riverhead Books, Penguin Putnam.

The Road Less Traveled: A New Psychology of Love, Traditional Values, and Spiritual Growth by M. Scott Peck, M.D. New York, 1985: Simon and Schuster.

The Selected Poetry of Edna St. Vincent Millay, Nancy Mitford, Editor. New York, 1971: Modern Library, div of Random House.

The Seven Habits of Highly Effective People, by Stephen Covey. New York, 1990: Simon & Schuster.

Shaken Faith: Hanging In There When God Seems Far Away by Antoinette Bosco. Mystic, CT, 2001: Twenty-Third Publications.

Surrender: Your Way to Spiritual Health and Freedom by Mary Hynes, Ph.D. Cincinnati, OH, 1999: St. Anthony Messenger Press.

Transitions by William Bridges, Ph.D. Reading, MA, 1980: Addison-Wesley Publishing Company.

Web Sites

griefnet.org offers is an Internet community of persons dealing with grief, death, and major loss.

misschildren.org The M.I.S.S. Foundation is a nonprofit international organization providing immediate and ongoing support to grieving families.

shalomplace.com An Online Christian Spirituality Center providing a wide variety of resources, including spiritual direction over the Internet, to encourage and support Christian contemplative spirituality.

Barbara Bartocci is a popular freelance writer for *Woman's Day, Family Circle, Good Housekeeping, Reader's Digest,* and others. She is a motivational speaker, lecturing frequently on spirituality and self-growth, and also a marketing consultant and presentation trainer for several major corporations. This is Bartocci's fifth book, following *Nobody's Child Anymore, Midlife Awakenings, Unexpected Answers,* and *My Angry Son.* Bartocci lives in a suburb of Kansas City.